A Short Dictionary of the Psalms

Jean-Pierre Prévost

translated by Mary Misrahi

A Liturgical Press Book

THE LITURGICAL PRESS
Collegeville, Minnesota

Cover design by David Manahan, O.S.B.

This book was first published by Editions du CERF under the title *Petit Dictionnaire des Psaumes,* ISSN 0222-9714 © CERF/S.B.E.V. (volume 71 of Cahier Evangile).

1	2	3	4	5	6	7	8	9

Library of Congress Cataloging-in-Publication Data

Prévost, Jean Pierre.
   [Petit dictionnaire des Psaumes.   English]
   A short dictionary of the Psalms / Jean-Pierre Prévost ; translated by Mary Misrahi.
     p.   cm.
   ISBN 0-8146-2370-0
   1. Bible. O.T. Psalms—Concordances, English. 2. Bible. O.T. Psalms—Language, style. 3. Bible. O.T. Psalms— Devotional use. 4. Bible. O.T. Psalms—Liturgical use. 5. Hebrew language—Glossaries, vocabularies, etc. I. Title.
BS1434.P7413   1997
223'.20447—dc21   96-36930
                                             CIP

Contents

Table (Hebrew-English)

Foreword

The original French version of this book is the third work on the psalms in a series. This third is perhaps more simple, and at any rate more practical. Jean-Pierre Prévost, a Montfort father who teaches at the University of St. Paul in Ottawa, thought up the idea of this short dictionary of the psalms. Out of the experience of numerous courses, seminars, and retreats he was able to fine-tune the explanations of vocabulary particular to these prayers of Israel, which have also become prayers of the Church.

Can the psalm found in the Sunday liturgy after the first reading truly nourish our prayer, at least as it is utilized today? It is our hope that this book can help today's Christians who pray the psalms—in particular those priests, religious, and laypersons who recite daily the Liturgy of the Hours—to return to the sources of these ancient inspired texts and thereby understand them better, penetrating more easily into this great school of prayer and the interior life that the Church has received from Israel.

There is no lack of problems, however: "We do not know how to pray as we ought!" St. Paul was already lamenting. The psalms reveal a mentality that is far from ours: this type of ancient poetry is so different from our modern life, the cult of the Temple that the psalms originally were a part of no longer exists, etc. In a word, everything conspires to make the psalms foreign to us. And yet, the ancient tree's sap still rises to nourish the youngest and most tender branches, for it is still the same Spirit who inspires these words and who shapes our being, psalm after psalm, down across the years.

Philippe Gruson

Introduction

Who is there among us who has not been deeply moved by the prayer of the psalms? They seem to move in to keep us company at the most significant moments of our lives. At times of great joy, alleluias and exclamations of gratitude come spontaneously to our lips: "O taste and see that the LORD is good!" (34:8), and "Give thanks to the LORD for he is good;/ for his steadfast love endures forever" (106:1). When we enjoy moments of great confidence have we not all hummed the refrain "The LORD is my shepherd, I shall not want" (23:1)? And in our darkest hours no words better express the suffering of the faithful than the opening words of Psalm 130: "Out of the depths I cry to you, O LORD./ Lord, hear my voice!" (v. 1).

The psalms have deeply influenced, and continue to influence, Jewish and Christian prayer. An inexhaustible treasure-house, they express joy as well as anguish, confidence as well as fear, the yearning for happiness as well as the fear of failure. They burst with life, but they also know the hatred and violence that are so rife throughout the world. As the remarkable source of prayer for Jews and Christians that they are, the psalms again and again turn our hearts to praise of God, while at the same time constantly calling to mind the plight of the wretched of the world who struggle daily for their rights and dignity, their survival and happiness.

Can the Psalms Be Our Prayer?

But are the psalms truly *our* prayer? As Christians who find ourselves praying the psalms on a daily basis, are we really as pleased as all that to have inherited this body of prayer from biblical tradition? A simple test will give us the answer. All we have to do is go back to our last Eucharistic Sunday assembly: How great an impact did the psalm have? In many instances, I am afraid the answer must be: not much of an impact at all.

It seems to be a fact that the psalm in our liturgical assemblies poses some difficulties, despite—or perhaps because of—its rich past. Summing up the situation, I am almost tempted to exclaim: "Poor psalm!" I have often heard the remark: "The psalm means nothing to our people." And the result is that we give in, we more or less read it, or we simply leave it out and substitute some other chant. The question of the music is a problem, but even more than that there is a fundamental problem concerning its placement: it is not clear what the psalm has to do either with the reading that preceded it (usually from the Old Testament) and with the reading of the Gospel that follows, and, even more importantly, what connection it provides between the two. Obviously, if the first reading were skipped, it would be no wonder if the psalm did not have an impact! And are there still sermons given that draw on the psalm text that was read or sung? So does the psalm really constitute part of the Liturgy of the Word? Or have the psalms lost all their power for us as the Word of God?

Frequent praying of the psalms constantly carries us into foreign territory. Their geography takes us into a very particular environment, the rural and desert-like Near East. Here we find bulls of Bashan (22:12) or jackals of the desert (44:19); we find ourselves suddenly sharing Shechem and roaming through the valley of Succoth (60:6); and the voice of God is heard as far as the wilderness of Kadesh (29:8). This is not the world we live in. Either we give up trying to truly understand and just say the words with no thought for their meaning, or we decide to look up the strange terms and try to find the equivalent in our own words.

The cultic backdrop, which occupies such a large place in the psalms, is yet another problem. The holocausts, the "odor of sweetness" of the rams, the blood of the bulls, the fattened beasts, all belong to the religious world of the ancient Near East and hold little attraction for our modern liturgies. We can of course find a spiritual symbolism for, say, the holocausts, but it is clear that for a Jew of the time of Isaiah, for instance, the word contained some very concrete resonances.

x   *takes us to historical Context.*

the language is not modern

Finally, the psalms set before us certain images of God that can at times get in the way or that fall short of the idea of the God revealed to us by Jesus Christ. No sooner does a group get together to study and reflect upon the psalms than the objection rises, before any other difficulty encountered in them, that God appears as a warrior, violent and vengeful. No matter how hard we work at explaining this difficulty away, countering it with the answer that it is not all that is said about God in the psalms, the problem does not go away. There remains a list of undigestible war-like epithets of God: fortress, shield, rampart, warrior, etc. "Contend, O LORD, with those who contend with me;/ fight against those who fight against me!/ Take hold of shield and buckler,/ and rise up to help me!/ Draw the spear and javelin/ against my pursuers" (35:1-3). Such a representation of God is a far cry from the evangelical precepts on imitating a God of mercy, on love of one's enemies, and on turning the other cheek. Even the beautiful and classic phrase "The Lord is my shepherd" is not always understood by people who have spent their whole lives in the city and who have probably never seen a flock of sheep, much less a shepherd caring for them!

For us as Christians, trying to pray the psalms two thousand years after they were written, a certain effort is necessary to make them ours, even at the cost of some discipline. Only then can we experience all their richness; only then can we confront them, enter into dialogue with them, and then go beyond their limitations to a level of prayer that is specifically Christian. It is up to us to draw from them something new and something old.

The Words That Express the Prayer of the Psalms

This little volume aims at helping us enter the world of the Psalter through the gateway of the specific words that constitute the characteristic vocabulary of the psalms. The idea is to provide a simple and concrete tool to help us savor the psalms and take them in more readily in all their distinctness. As I turned to the enormous and exceedingly rich literature on the Psalter, I became convinced that there was still room left for such a tool, taking up where the more technical works of research leave off. By means of the explanation of certain key words, such a tool would help all those who are exposed to the psalms enter more readily into their theological and spiritual worlds.

From the point of view of its vocabulary, the case of the Psalter is entirely unique. First of all, there is the great amount of repetition. The prayer vocabulary here is not extensive; the same words are used over and over again. This in itself tells us something: we should not look for inventiveness or elegance of speech in prayer, but rather the truth of personal relationship. The words themselves are there just to get the dialogue going, a jumping-off place for communication. They are not the essence of the prayer, which lies in the relationship they presuppose and are there to deepen.

Then there is the question of the original language of the psalms—Hebrew—which has its own genius that we do not always manage to convey in our modern translations. Hebrew is extraordinarily compact, especially Hebrew poetry (and the psalms are poetry), and it characteristically proceeds by strongly contrasting oppositions. An example: "For the LORD watches over the way of the righteous,/ but the way of the wicked will perish" (1:6). We need eighteen words to translate what only took eight in Hebrew!

Also, Hebrew is a language constructed from roots. For example, the word *miqdash,* which means temple, implies a relationship with the sacred because it is made from the root *qodesh.* While it is true that in our languages we can find a logical connection between temple and sacredness, it is nevertheless not at all apparent from the words themselves.

A third characteristic of Hebrew, and one that flows naturally from the preceding, is the polyvalence of words. The same Hebrew word can have four or five different translations. For example, the word *chesed* can be translated as loving-kindness, love, goodness, tenderness, loyalty, and faithfulness. While these can all be considered similar in that they are all eminently good qualities, there is nevertheless an appreciable difference between, for example, tenderness and faithfulness. So in order to understand the psalms and have some inner experience of the spirit in which they were written, it seems that we must grasp these different nuances of meaning.

Forty Key Words

A vocabulary of forty words was selected out of the many possible. For each of these words all its usages were verified and studied. They were chosen largely because of their frequency, but also because of the diversity of meanings that they might assume for our modern mentalities.

The individual entries under the modern meaning were made according to the translation most often used in the Psalter for the particular Hebrew root. The equivalent in Hebrew is given immediately underneath, both in transliteration and in Hebrew characters. The statistics given usually refer to the number of occurrences of all words based on that particular root.[1] However, for fifteen or so of the key words, it seemed preferable to consider only one word, or a few words, drawn from that root. In these cases, the box at the right supplies the cumulative total of all uses of the "other forms" of the root. The box itself has as its title (in transliteration) the form of the root or of the derived words most often encountered. In most cases, this will be the verb in the simple conjugation. The box then supplies the statistics: first, the total occurrences of the word or the root in the Old Testament, then the comparative frequency of its occurrence in the different books. Given first are the three books in which it occurs most often, with respective totals. In cases where the book of Psalms is not one of these three, that statistic is also given, allowing us to see at a glance the position of the Psalter in relation to the other books, as well as the number of times the word or root occurs in the psalms.

The word study is done on the original Hebrew, but a table in two parts given at the beginning of the book will allow those who know no Hebrew to refer easily to the words and themes from their equivalent in the English.

Each of the articles is divided into two sections. The first section gives etymological and semantic information on the meaning of the root and the words compounded from it. The second section is devoted almost exclusively to the use of the word or the root in the Psalter, and it will attempt to identify its characteristic meanings. A series of separate essays throughout this volume provide helpful information serving as a general introduction to the Psalter that will hopefully help the reader with some problems that may be encountered when using the psalms as prayer in today's world.

1. The statistics relative to the Hebrew text were established with the help of the computer (using The Perfect Word). The results were compared with what was available in the Concordances (among others, Mandelkern) and the classic dictionaries of the Old Testament (e.g., Jenni-Westermann), and any necessary changes were made.

BLESS
BARAK   ברך

Barak	
Total OT	398
1. Gen	88
2. Ps	83
3. Deut	51

1. Root

There are two *barak* roots in Hebrew and in the other ancient Semitic languages, one meaning to kneel (see Ps 95:6) and the other to bless. There is perhaps a connection between the two, for the knee is sometimes used as a euphemism for the sex organ, and the blessing most desired from God is fertility.

The prayer for blessing is the most frequently used in the Bible (there are 398 such prayers), and it is undoubtedly the most characteristic form of Jewish prayer. Jews pray daily the "Eighteen Blessings," and there are extensive prayers of blessing at the beginning of each of the major liturgical services. The blessing is an ancient form of prayer that is often encountered in the stories of the patriarchs as a spontaneous form of prayer in the home. In the Psalter the verb *barak* is found seventy-four times, and the noun *berakah* nine times.

2. Usage

In contrast to the prayers of blessing long dominant in our churches, blessings in the Bible are usually conferred upon people (very rarely on things or material objects) and are directed more toward God than to people. It is God who is blessed, rather than we: "Blessed be the LORD" (28:6; 31:21; 41:13; etc.).

As a prayer of thanksgiving, the blessing was inspired by certain concrete circumstances where the action of God has been particularly favorable: "I bless the LORD who gives me counsel" (16:7); "Blessed be the LORD/ for he has heard the sound of my pleadings" (28:6); "Blessed be the LORD,/ for he has wondrously shown his steadfast love to me/ when I was beset as a city under siege" (31:21); "Blessed be the LORD,/ who has not given us/ as prey to their teeth" (124:6).

Although it occurs less frequently, the blessing of God is given to humanity some 30 times in the Psalter. First, the earth

1

is blessed with a series of divine actions to ensure its fecundity: "You visit the earth and water it,/ . . . You water its furrows abundantly,/ . . . softening it with showers,/ and blessing its growth" (65:9-10); "I will abundantly bless its provisions;/ I will satisfy its poor with bread" (132:15). And the blessing of divine protection is invoked upon the people: "O save your people, and bless your heritage" (28:9); "May the LORD bless his people with peace!" (29:11); "May God be gracious to us and bless us/ and make his face to shine upon us" (67:1); "The LORD has been mindful of us; he will bless us" (115:12). Finally, blessing is bestowed upon individuals, who are comforted by God's presence and overwhelmed with God's favors: "For you bless the righteous, O LORD;/ you cover them with favor as with a shield" (5:12); "You bestow on him [the king] blessings forever;/ you make him glad with the joy of your presence" (21:6).

BREATH
RUACH רוח

Ruach	
Total OT	378
1. Ezek	52
2. Isa	51
3. Ps	39
Other Forms	11

1. Root

The dictionaries give us two different roots, related to each other, as the etymology of *ruach:* either the verb *rawach*, which means to be spacious, to be light (e.g., 1 Sam 16:23), or the verb *riach*, which means to breathe in, to smell (e.g., Ps 115:6). The latter is more commonly held among the commentators. Aside from the verb form, used only in the causative conjugation (eleven times in the Old Testament), the noun *reach* is also found (odor, fragrance; 58 times in the Old Testament).

2. Usage

Western cultures tend to link the spirit to the mind and intelligence, but for the biblical authors the connotation is, on the contrary, much closer to the vital functions of the will and the emotions. It may very well be best to keep the literal translation of breath,[1] which preserves a certain indefiniteness and openness to a variety of translations. We can understand *ruach* as the breath of the wind, (Gen 1:2; 3:8; Exod 14:21; Ps 1:4; 18:11, 43), as the physical breath of animals (Gen 7:15; Ps 104:29) or of humans (Judg 15:19; Isa 42:5; Eccl 12:7; Ps 31:6; 146:4), or, finally, as the breath of God (Isa 30:1; 42:1; 44:3; Ezek 36:27; 37:14; 39:29; etc.).

In the case of the Psalter, breath is certainly the best translation for *ruach,* for it lends itself to both the cosmic and the anthropological dimensions of the word (found 15x. with the sense of wind, and just as often with the meaning of the breath of life of human beings). The psalmists speak of the wind that raises and blows dust (Ps 18:43) or chaff (1:4; 83:14), the fearful wind of the storm and the hurricane (55:9; 107:25; 148:8), and the beneficial wind that brings the rain and makes the earth fruitful (135:7).

Breath is the very life of humans: "When you take away their breath, they die/ and return to their dust./ When you send forth your spirit, they are created" (104:29-30). How precious is this breath of life, absolutely indispensable, and yet so fragile: "He remembered that they were but flesh,/ a wind that passes and does not come again" (78:39). It is also in the *ruach* that plans and decisions are made: "Happy are those . . . in whose spirit there is no deceit" (32:2). Both courage and human vitality are nourished or, on the contrary, lost in the realm of the spirit: "Restore to me the joy of your salvation,/ and sustain in me a willing spirit" (51:12); "The LORD is near to the brokenhearted,/ and saves the crushed in spirit" (34:18); "When my spirit is faint,/ you know my way" (142:3); "Therefore my spirit faints within me;/ my heart within me is appalled" (143:4). To entrust one's breath to God is much more than giving intellectual assent; it is the total giving over of one's life into God's hands: "Into your hand I commit my spirit" (31:5; see also Luke 23:46).

Imbued with the initial vision of Genesis (Gen 1:2), the psalmists see in the breath of God a force that gives life to all of creation: "By the word of the LORD the heavens were made,/ and all their host by the breath of his mouth" (33:6);

"He sends out his word, and melts them;/ he makes his wind blow, and the waters flow" (147:18). In God's breath is a mystery of holiness ("do not take your holy spirit from me," 51:11) and of goodness ("Teach me to do your will. . . ./ Let your good spirit lead me on a level path," 143:10).

1. See André Myre, *Un souffle subversif* (Montreal: Bellarmin, 1988) 160.

CALL (CRY OUT TO)

QARA' קרא

Qara'	
Total OT	730
1. Gen	105
2. Isa	62
3. Ps	56
Other forms	29

1. Root

The verb *qara'* essentially means call, but with all the nuances of meaning that this verb can imply: call together (convoke), invite, give a name to, invoke, cry out to. In the Psalter the last meaning stands out. Of the ninety-some places in the Bible where this verb has the meaning of crying out to God, a little more than half (47) are found in the psalms.

2. Usage

The prayer of the psalms devotes a large share to the different cries that arise spontaneously in the human heart in situations of distress (4:1; 50:15; 86:7; 102:2; 120:1), of anguish (18:6; 34:6; 118:5), of discouragement (61:2), of humiliation (31:17), of persecution (3:4; 17:6; 18:3; 56:9), and of suffering that can lead to death (30:9; 88:9).

The way this verb is used clearly underscores the nature of the prayer of the psalms as a dialogue between two parties. In fact, in some twenty verses a verb of response or listening is paired with it: "I cry aloud to the LORD,/ and he answers me from his holy hill" (3:4); "Answer me when I call, O God of my right" (4:1); "The LORD hears when I call to him" (4:2); "I call upon you, for you will answer me, O God;/ incline your ear to me, hear my words" (17:6). No matter how loud and heart-rending the cries that arise in the human heart may be, they are never despairing. In fact, they would not be so loud if they did not have the certitude of being heard: "The poor soul cried, and was heard by the LORD" (34:6).

But sometimes it happens that one's hope is sorely tried, and one's insistent cries seem to go unanswered: "O my God, I cry by day, but you do not answer;/ and by night, but find no rest" (22:2); "I am weary with my crying;/ my throat is parched./ My eyes grow dim/ with waiting for my God" (69:3). The dark night of faith is filled with doubts, but they will not last forever: Psalms 22 and 69 end unequivocally with an act of thanksgiving. At the end of the long night of silence, God has finally answered!

The cry in itself is enough to draw the attention of God. But it must be supported by the life of the faithful in order to bear fruit: "If I had cherished iniquity in my heart,/ the Lord would not have listened" (66:18); "The LORD is near to all who call on him,/ to all who call on him in truth./ He fulfills the desire of all who fear him" (145:18-19). Even in the midst of trials, the dignity of the faithful before God is preserved, and the cry of supplication turns into one of praise: "I cried aloud to him,/ and he was extolled with my tongue" (66:17).

More rarely, the psalms speak of the cry or call of God. It is a call that creates; it illustrates the extent of divine power over the created universe: "He determines the number of the stars;/ he gives to all of them their names" (147:4). But there is another sense, an awe-inspiring one, to the word. God convokes all the earth as witness at the trial of God's people: "The mighty one, God the LORD,/ speaks and summons the earth/ from the rising of the sun to its setting./ He calls to the heavens above/ and to the earth, that he may judge his people" (50:1, 4).

DAVID   דָּוִד

David	
Total OT	1,075
1. 1 Sam	291
2. 2 Sam	285
3. 1 Chr	189
5. Ps	88

1. David, the Author of the Psalms?

The figure of David remains of capital importance for understanding the psalms. Aside from the historical books that cover his reign, his name appears most often in the Psalter. And of the eighty-eight references, seventy-three are found as headings, the superscriptions, or subtitles of individual psalms. The formula in Hebrew is *"mizmor leDavid"* (sometimes reversed), which is ambiguous in that it could mean either "psalm for (in honor of) David" or "psalm by David." Moreover, at the end of Psalm 72 we find that a collection of psalms is attributed to him: "The prayers of David son of Jesse are ended" (72:20). Every time his name is used it is to attribute the composition to him.

On one hand, the attribution is legitimate and fits in well with the real historical role of David in the development of the liturgy, especially of the psalms. The ancient historical books (e.g., 2 Sam 6:23) already alluded to this role of David, and it is acknowledged throughout biblical tradition, especially in the later books of the Old Testament (1 Chr 15:16; 16:7; 23; Sir 47:8-10).

On the other hand, we must not be overly credulous about these attributions. A good number of the mentions speak of David in the third person or qualify him with a title he would probably not have given himself (see Psalms 3; 7; 18; 34; 36; etc.). Linguistic criteria point in another direction entirely, to the post-exilic period (see the box insert on "The Dating of the Psalms: A Long Story").

2. The Psalms and David's Experience

The Psalter has more and better things to say about David than mere attribution: David is the man and the believer, conscious of and unhappy about his limitations, his sins, and his anguish, or, on the contrary, aware of the loving kindness of the Lord and rejoicing in it. In fact, no less than fourteen psalms can be imputed to a particular episode, sometimes well-known, sometimes obscure, of David's life (3; 7; 18; 34; 36; 51; 52; 54; 56; 57; 59; 60; 63; 142). In those cases where the episode is familiar, the psalm clearly gains in human depth. This is particularly true of Psalm 51, which is evocative without being accusatory: "A psalm of David, when the prophet Nathan came to him, after he had gone in to Bathsheba." In it we find the personification of the forgiven sinner, assuming full responsibility for his sins and becoming a "new creature" through the tenderness and mercy of God.

3. David as a Messianic Figure

Finally, every time David's name is invoked in the body of a psalm, he is given the character of a theological symbol, an heir of the promise ("I have made a covenant with my chosen one,/ I have sworn to my servant David:/ 'I will establish your descendants forever,/ and build your throne for all generations,'" 89:3-4), or as the figure of the Messiah ("I have found my servant David;/ with my holy oil I have anointed him," 89:20), chosen to be the shepherd of his people (78:70-72; see also 18:51; 89:36-37; 132:10-11, 17; 144:10).

FEAR

YARE⁾ ירא

Yare⁾	
Total OT	435
1. Ps	83
2. Deut	44
3. Isa	34

1. Root

The root *yare⁾* appears in the verb (333x., including the 45 uses of the participle *nora⁾*, fearsome, and the same number for the verbal adjective *yare⁾*, fearing) as well as in the two nouns for fear: *yir⁾ah* (45x.) and *mora⁾* (12x.).

Basically, the root applies to all the different emotions arising from a state of fear. In the religious sphere, however, it takes on a special connotation closer to what we call reverence, that is, that particular attitude of respect for the mystery of God.

2. Usage

Fear arises from a real danger, which the psalmists try to overcome. Even when they tell us that they have vanquished their fears, they reveal what they were concerned about. For example, the psalmists feared times of trouble (49:5) or simply evil tidings (112:7), the terror of the night (91:5), the evil in the darkest valley (23:4), the threatening ten thousands of people (3:6) or the blows inflicted by flesh (56:4), by mere mortals (56:11; 118:6).

The fear of God also means just that—God is fearsome and feared, God inspires fear: "But you indeed are awesome!/ Who can stand before you/ when once your anger is roused?/ From the heavens you uttered judgment;/ the earth feared and was still" (76:7-8); "Who considers the power of your anger?/ Your wrath is as great as the fear that is due you" (90:11); "My flesh trembles for fear of you,/ and I am afraid of your judgments" (119:120). No matter how we might wish to soften the impact of these texts, it remains a fact that fear plays a certain role in the religion of Israel, and in ours as well (see the writings of Jean Delumeau).

The most noticeable use of the root in the psalms is the frequently occurring verbal adjective those who fear you (4x.), those who fear him (10x.), those who fear the Lord (6x.), those who fear God (once). Who are these persons who fear God? They are actually the community of believers. They are the liturgical assembly, gathered at the Temple to give glory to God: "You who fear the LORD, praise him!/ From you comes my praise in the great congregation;/ my vows I will pay before those who fear him" (22:23, 25). It would seem that in the more recent texts the term came to specifically mean the pious: "The friendship of the LORD is for those who fear him,/ and he makes his covenant known to them" (25:14; see also 34:10; 103:11, 13). The one who fears God seems to be the exemplar of the believer, the ideal believer, the one who walks in his ways (128:1).

In the presence of the divine, the people of the Bible developed an acute sense of the distance between God and themselves: God is the utterly other. From this perspective, the fear of God is a perfectly normal and healthy reaction. It is, precisely, that sense of the mystery of God, the respect and awe before God's otherness. It is adoration. But such fear in no way instils the anguished emotions associated with anger. It is just the opposite, a source of blessing and happiness: "Happy are those who fear the LORD" (112:1; see also 128:1).

FLESH

BASAR   בשר

Basar	
Total OT	270
1. Lev	61
2. Gen	33
3. Job	18
4. Ps	16

1. Root

This word occurs in other Semitic languages with the sense of flesh or body. It is found in almost all the books of the Old Testament. However, it is not used frequently in the Psalter. Body and flesh have acquired a Greek sense in Western Christian tradition that is totally absent from the biblical viewpoint (see the word Soul).

2. Usage

There is a physical dimension to prayer in the psalms. Physical emotions are part and parcel of the psalmist's prayer, and there is never a tendency to escape from the realities of the flesh for some purely spiritual world: "There is no soundness in my flesh/ because of your indignation" (38:3); "My flesh faints for you,/ as in a dry and weary land where there is no water" (63:1); "Because of my loud groaning/ my bones cling to my skin" (102:5); "My flesh trembles for fear of you" (119:120).

The psalmists use the term "all flesh" when referring to all of humanity (65:2; 136:25). They also use the word to distinguish between God and us: God has a *nefesh* and a *ruach*, but not a *basar*. It is not until the prologue of the Gospel of John that we hear the incredible news: the Word (= God) became flesh *(basar)*! But until then there was no better way to depict the great barrier that separates humans from God than by invoking this essential difference: Humankind possesses flesh, fragile and vulnerable. Happily, this difference is taken account of and pleads, so to speak, in our favor. God remembers that we are flesh and hastens to pardon: "Yet he, being compassionate,/ forgave their iniquity,/ and did not destroy them. . . ./ He remembered that they were but flesh,/ a wind that passes and does not come again" (78:38-39).

What is this flesh or this body that this idea could so clearly mark the difference between God and us? When the Bible speaks of *basar*, the meaning is that of human finitude, fragility, vulnerability. When the psalmists speak of the flesh they are not making a negative or suspicious judgment about sexuality, for instance. They are simply recognizing the fact that we are limited. This is a fact, a reality, that we must accept joyously and without resignation. All of us, women and men, with all our limitations, are called together to sing the glory of the Lord: "All flesh will bless his holy name forever and ever" (145:21).

The sense is clear: flesh is not something that has been slapped on top of us, something exterior and marginal, so to speak. In the biblical view of things, the soul is not (as Plato thought) the prisoner of the body. The body, the flesh, is what we are. Here we have the great difference between biblical anthropology and Greek anthropology, for example, where there was the tendency to distinguish, if not to actually oppose, the body and the soul, matter and spirit. In the mind of the psalmists we form a whole, unified, incapable of being broken down into components. Everything is bound up in one: "My soul longs, indeed it faints/ for the courts of the Lord;/ my heart and my flesh sing for joy/ to the living God" (84:2).

The Dating of the Psalms: A Long Story

Dating the psalms is a difficult and risky business. Even the titles and subscripts that attribute the psalm to an individual (such as David) or refer it to a particular episode of his life are not above suspicion. What can be said with certitude is that the composition of the Psalter was spread out over a longer period than any other book of the Bible—almost a thousand years. Here are the principal facts of this long history.

1. The oldest psalms are not found in the Psalter. These are Exodus 15 and Judges 5, at least some passages of which are to be dated as contemporary with the experience they relate (the time of Moses and the time of the Judges).

2. David (who reigned between 1000 and 970 B.C.E.) and his collaborators were responsible, according to the Bible, for the organization of the liturgical life of Israel and for the creation of the psalms, as well as for collecting them together (see 1 Chronicles 15–16; 25; Sir 47:8-10).

3. The canonical prophets (in particular Jeremiah, in the seventh century B.C.E.) had a great influence on the Psalter (see, e.g., Psalm 1, which takes up the theme of Jer 17:5-8). In those cases where there is a clear affinity between a prophetic text and a psalm, the consensus of scholars is to make the psalm derive from the prophetic passage, and not the reverse. It certainly would not make much sense for a prophet, by nature so personally involved and so radically innovative, to repeat a well-known and time-worn refrain from a psalm familiar to mostly everyone. But the reverse is

quite believable: the tradition of the psalms rested firmly on the authority of the prophets.

4. The experience of the Exile and the Return (597–538 B.C.E.) appears frequently in the psalms (13:7; the end lines of 51; most of 126 and 137; 147:2-3). A good number of psalms reflect the dismay of Israel during those dark days, as well as their wild joy upon their return.

5. A certain number of psalms seem to refer to a crisis comparable to that of the Exile, but at the same time lament the absence of all prophecy (74:9; 77:9-10; 83; 89:6-8). This leads us to infer that they were composed during the Maccabean period (around 160 B.C.E.), when the decline of prophecy was much deplored (Dan 3:38; 1 Macc 9:27).

In summary, the history of the psalms is extremely rich and complex. Those collected into the Psalter cover a period of some eight hundred years. In practice, each psalm has to be studied individually, in its vocabulary and its theology, and compared with other biblical texts whose date is more certain.

The fruit of such a long history, the psalms are Israel's faithful companion par excellence. They reflect Israel's hours of glory in all their exaltation, as well as the crises so disturbing to the people's faith. As a melting-pot of the various theological traditions of Israel, the psalms must be considered a summary of the theological and spiritual faith of the Old Testament.

GLORY

KAVOD כבוד

Kavod	
Total OT	200
1. Ps	151
2. Isa	38
3. Ezek	19
Other Forms	176

1. Root

The noun *kavod* is derived from an intransitive verb *(kaved)* that means to have weight, to be heavy: "For day and night your hand was heavy upon me" (32:4); "For my iniquities have gone over my head;/ they weigh like a burden too heavy for me" (38:4). The basic idea is that of weight or density. This makes the meaning of glory in the Bible not one of reputation and renown, which is reflected back from the outside upon a person; it arises rather from the interior weight or density of a person, the weight of his or her presence and actions.

2. Usage

There is only 1 occurrence of purely human glory, and then it means riches: "Do not be afraid when some become rich,/ when the wealth of their houses increases./ For when they die they will carry nothing [no *kavod*] away" (49:16-17).

In many instances the glory is that which the person finds in God: "But you, O LORD, are a shield around me,/ my glory, and the one who lifts up my head" (3:3); "On God rests my deliverance and my honor" (62:7); "You guide me with your counsel,/ and afterward you will receive me with honor" (73:24); "For the LORD God is a sun and shield;/ he bestows favor and honor./ No good thing does the LORD withhold/ from those who walk uprightly" (84:11). We are not to seek glory in wealth or power, but in God, whose very presence gives stability and weight to everything that exists in the universe. To give the real meaning of glory, then, we really should speak of presence. The glory of God is the radiant manifestation of God's being: "On the glorious splendor of your majesty,/ and on your wondrous works,/ I will meditate" (145:5). To speak of the glory of God is to speak of God's radiance in the world, God's self-manifestation outside the reign of heaven, and, finally, of God's presence and dwelling in the world: "The heavens are telling the glory of God;/ and the firmament proclaims his handiwork" (19:1); "O LORD, I love the house in which you dwell,/ and the place where your glory abides" (26:8); "Surely his salvation is at hand for those who fear him,/ that his glory may dwell in our land" (85:9).

Psalm 24 celebrates Yahweh as the king of glory (vv. 7-10). Glory is a divine attribute, linked to the power and holiness of God: "Ascribe to the LORD, O heavenly beings,/ ascribe to the LORD glory and strength./ Ascribe to the LORD the glory of his name;/ worship the LORD in holy splendor" (29:1-2; see also 96:7-8); "So I have looked upon you in the sanctuary,/ beholding your power and glory" (63:2). Another aspect of the glory of God is that it extends to the ends of the universe: "Be exalted, O God, above the heavens./ Let your glory be over all the earth" (57:5, 11; see also 108:6; 113:4).

The prayer of Israel, in community or in private, is attentive to the diverse manifestations of the glory of God. For Israel, to give glory to God is simply to acknowledge God's greatness, to be open to God's presence, and to be able to perceive the splendor of God throughout the world: "All the nations you have made shall come/ and bow down before you, O Lord,/ and shall glorify your name" (86:9); "I will glorify your name forever" (86:12).

GOD (NAMES OF)

Since the entire Psalter can be considered a cry to God, it is not surprising that the divine names occupy an important place in the psalms. They tell us something about the being to whom the psalmists addressed their prayer, and reveal the God they sought and found, called upon in distress and doubt, and accepted in faith and love. If we limit ourselves to the seven names of God (Yahweh, ʾEl, ʾElohim, ʾEloah, ʾAdonai, ʾElyon, and Shaddai), there are 1,275 references to God, some eight per psalm.

Yahweh

This is the divine name that is, not surprisingly, used the most often: 695 times in its complete form, and 43 times in the abridged *Yah* (as in Allelu*IA*). This is the highest total for any book of the Old Testament. The section of Psalms 42–72 uses this name less often (only 30 times), but emphasizes rather ʾElohim (164x.); for this reason we can speak of an "elohist Psalter" for Psalms 42–72, the second book.

The fact that Yahweh is used most frequently in the Psalter allows us to affirm that the God of the psalmists is above all the personal God revealed to Moses ("I AM WHO I AM," Exod 3:14). This was the God who was revealed through decisive intervention in Egypt on behalf of an oppressed people, a God forever present who accompanies the people as a community, as well as individuals.

From before the third century B.C.E., Jews have evinced such respect for this primary name for God that they will never pronounce it aloud, always substituting another name for it. Similarly, this respect has led to the substitution of the name Lord for Yahweh in many modern translations. In the New Revised Standard Edition the name is printed in small capitals: LORD.

Three attributes of the face of Yahweh are particularly striking in the psalms. Yahweh is great: "O LORD, our Sovereign,/ how majestic is your name in all the earth!" (8:1); "Great is the LORD and greatly to be praised" (48:1; see also 96:4). This greatness implies that we acknowledge the unfathomable mystery of God. But God is also, in the full meaning of the term, unique: "For who is God except the LORD?/ And who is a rock besides our God?" (18:31); "Let them know that you alone,/ whose name is the LORD,/ are the Most High over all the earth" (83:18); "O LORD God of hosts,/ who is as mighty as you, O LORD?" (89:8); "Who is like the LORD our God?" (113:5). With refrains like these the psalmists insist again and again on the monotheistic faith of Israel. Yahweh alone is God! And finally, the psalms speak of a God who is good and full of love: "O give thanks to the LORD, for he is good" (107:1; 136:1); "But you, O Lord, are a God merciful and gracious,/ slow to anger and abounding in steadfast love and faithfulness" (86:15); "For the LORD is good;/ his steadfast love endures forever,/ and his faithfulness to all generations" (100:5).

We can say, with Evode Beaucamp, that the name of Yahweh has in the prayer of the Old Testament the importance that the name Father has in the prayer of Jesus and Christians. "When Israel called upon Yahweh, when Christians say 'Father,' they are both expressing all that they hoped for in advance from the God of the Covenant, both the old and the new."[1]

ʾEl, ʾElohim, ʾEloah

The name ʾEl for God is not used by Israel alone. It is an ancient name inherited from neighboring Semitic peoples. One possible etymology relates it to the root ʾol, to be powerful. The name ʾEl is used 238 times in the Old Testament, above all in the poetic books, which show a great affinity to each other in other ways as well: the Psalter (77x.), Job (55x.), and Isaiah (24x.). It is almost never found in the historical books (it is absent altogether from 1 and 2 Kings and 1 and 2 Chronicles), nor in the wisdom literature (only Job uses it). It is scarcely attested in the prophets aside from Isaiah. But ʾEl plays a big part in the religion of the patriarchs: Abraham and Jacob encountered ʾEl at Bethel (Gen 12:8; 35:1-7); ʾEl was worshiped at Beersheba under the name ʾEl ʿOlam (Gen 21:33), at Shechem as the God of Israel (Gen 33:20), and at Jerusalem under the name of ʾEl ʿElyon (Gen 14:18-20).

Even though this name for God was supplanted later by the name Yahweh revealed to Moses, it would be wrong to totally oppose these two names, when the psalmists and the bulk of the Old Testament constantly associate them and treat them as identical. Psalm 78, which is quite long (72 vv.), relates the story of Israel's salvation and lists the actions attributed traditionally to Yahweh, but it only mentions this name twice, preferring here the names ʾEl and ʾElohim (14x.).

ʾEl occurs often in the singular with the suffix of the first person singular (ʾEli, "my God"), which underscores the trust and intimacy that the psalmists feel when they address God (18:3; 22:2 [spoken by Jesus on the Cross]; 22:11; 63:2; 68:25; 89:27, etc.).

There is another name in the singular that the psalmists use to call upon God: ʾEloah. It appears four times in the Psalter (18:32; 50:22; 114:7; 139:19). The rest of the Old Testament rarely uses it: Job alone has forty-one of the fifty-seven times it appears in the entire Old Testament.

Lastly, the plural form ʾElohim appears second in frequency behind Yahweh among the divine names. Out of a total of

2,600 occurrences, Deuteronomy, Psalms, and Genesis hold the first three places, with 374, 365, and 219 respectively. The form is plural, and sometimes the meaning is also, since the word can be used to refer to the pagan gods or idols of neighboring peoples. But in most cases the plural form is followed by a verb or adjective in the singular, the explanation being that this plural expresses plenitude or transcendence.

ʾAdonai

The Psalter uses this name for God sixty-seven times, thus holding third place in frequency after Ezekiel (222x.) and Genesis (80x.). The name ʾAdon or ʾAdonai, which came to be used when Yahweh is written, out of respect for the name of God, comes from the world of domestic relationships. It referred to the master (owner of a home) who had servants at his command. In the ancient Near East it was also used to express the authority of the king over those who dwelled in his territory.

The psalms use the term in both senses. Psalm 86 gives a good illustration of the first, domestic sense: in a private supplication full of confidence, the psalmist calls God his master no less than seven times (possibly to give the impression of plenitude; vv. 3-5, 8, 9, 12, 15). He refers to himself as servant (vv. 2, 4, 16). In itself, the term does not imply an insurmountable distance between the servant and the master, but rather that the servant belongs wholly to the master and is willing to serve. The second meaning of the term is used for an earthly king, prefiguring the Messiah in the famous Oracle of the Lord to my lord (110:1). It also refers to God, creator of the universe, whose kingship is based on that fact ("The LORD is king! Let the earth rejoice!/ The mountains melt like wax before the LORD,/ before the Lord of all the earth," 97:1, 5).

ʿElyon

This name is also found most frequently in the Psalter (21x. out of a total of 31). This word is an epithet, derived from the root ʿalah, which means to go up. Thus ʿElyon means raised up or elevated. The idea of elevation expresses doubtlessly the high places where God dwells, but it also refers to God's preeminence among the other gods: "For you, O LORD, are most high over all the earth;/ you are exalted far above all gods"

(97:9). The use of this name is associated with the personage of Melchizedek (Gen 14:18-19) and remained linked with Zion-Jerusalem. It has a monarchical and royal connotation, fostering the celebration of God as king: "For the LORD, the Most High, is awesome,/ a great king over all the earth" (47:2).

Shaddai

This archaic name, often translated the Almighty, is found in two very old segments (Gen 49:25 and Num 24:4, 16 [the oracles of Balaam]) and is used in reference to the times of the patriarchs (in Exod 6:3 Yahweh reminds Moses that it is indeed under this name that God is revealed to them). It appears that this word refers to a mountain divinity. It is only found in the Psalter twice, in 68:15 and 91:1. Only the first of these resonates with the mountain aspect of Shaddai, by recalling what happened at Sinai, the sacred mountain (68:9), compared to the mount of Zion: "Why do you look with envy, O many-peaked mountain,/ at the mount that God desired for his abode/ where the LORD will reside forever?" (68:16). The second occurrence does not necessarily refer to the mountain aspect of Shaddai, but it does imply a place just as impregnable that can serve as a refuge: "You who live in the shelter of the Most High,/ who abide in the shadow of the Almighty,/ will say to the LORD, 'My refuge and my fortress;/ my God, in whom I trust'" (91:1-2).

1. É. Beaucamp, *Israël en prière. Des psaumes au Notre Père* (Paris: Cerf/Sigier, 1985) 11.

Occurrences of the Names of God		
	In the OT	*In the Pss*
Yahweh	6,828	695
Yah	50	43
ꞌEl	238	77
ꞌElohim	2,600	365
ꞌEloah	57	4
ꞌAdon/ai	773	67
ꞌElyon	31	21
Shaddai	48	2

GRACE
(FAVOR, PARDON,
MERCY)
CHANAN חָנַן

Chanan	
Total OT	223
1. Ps	56
2. Prov	26
3. Gen	19

1. Root

The root *chanan* appears most frequently in the Bible in the verb form (78x.) and as the noun *chen*, meaning grace, favor, pardon (69x.). There are two other related nouns used in the sense of supplication (begging for forgiveness): *techinnah* and *tachannunim* (43x. each). There is also an adjective, *channun* (gracious, forgiving), applied in twelve out of its thirteen occurrences to God. The Septuagint translates the word most often as the verb *ʾEleein* (to have pity), and the noun *chen* is always translated as *charis* (grace, favor).

The primary meaning of the root *chanan* refers to physical beauty: "You are the most handsome of men;/ grace is poured upon your lips" (45:2; see also Prov 11:16). The noun *chen* is most often used in a secular sense, meaning a concrete gesture of kindliness that has been freely given: "If I find favor with you" (Gen 33:10; 2 Sam 14:22; 16:4).

2. Usage

There is no theory of grace and forgiveness in the Psalter. *Chen* is used only twice, and then in the sense of beauty (45:2), paralleled with *glory* (84:12). The two other related nouns are preferred to *chen*, and they emphasize the character of supplication of the prayer of the psalms. The verb *chanan* does so even more; it occurs in a number of forms. So grace (favor, pardon) is not seen by the psalmists as an abstract reality. Its true meaning is grasped only in the context of an experience of the gratuitous nature of God's interventions.

The God of the psalmists is indeed the God of Exodus: "But you, O Lord, are a God merciful and gracious,/ slow to anger and abounding in steadfast love and faithfulness" (86:15; see

19

also 103:8; 111:4; 116:5; 145:8). God is a gracious and kindly God, who listens with favor to the cries of distress of the faithful. God also cannot be manipulated in any way, remaining a God of freedom and freely given graces.

The cry "Have pity on me/us" (*channeni* 17x., *channenu* twice) expresses the urgency of the prayer as well as the freedom of God to grant the pardon or not, as is God's will. The cry arises spontaneously to the lips of the psalmist in times of particular crisis (4:2; 6:3; 9:14; 25:16; 26:11; 27:7).

Grace and pardon are God's to give: in principle, it is always God who bestows pardon. But there are two interesting exceptions in the psalms. In the first case, it is the attitude of the just person who does not hesitate to freely give to the one who is in need: "The wicked borrow, and do not pay back,/ but the righteous are generous and keep giving./ They are ever giving liberally and lending" (37:21, 26). The other case is even more interesting. Clearly paraphrasing Exodus 34:6, the revelation of a loving God, the psalmist here sees the vocation of the just person in the sense of a participation in this divine kindliness: "They rise in the darkness as a light for the upright;/ they are gracious, merciful, and righteous" (112:4). The grace or pardon received from God is intended to be shared with others and must lead to an attitude of free pardon and mercy toward one's neighbor.

HAPPY

ᵓASHREI אשרי

	ᵓAshrei
Total OT	45
1. Ps	26
2. Prov	8
3. Isa	3

1. Root

The word translated as the adjective happy or blessed is, in fact, a plural noun in Hebrew. Literally, it ought to be translated as something like "blessings of." The precise etymology is uncertain. According to one explanation, the word *ᵓashrei* is derived from the verb to walk or move. The same root, *ʾashar*, means go or lead (see Isa 3:12; 9:15). In this case, happiness would be an essentially dynamic concept, always forging ahead, the object of hope and searching. Another possibility is that the word *ʾashrei* is derived from the root *yashar*, to be upright, to be just. The meaning then would be that just behavior toward others would result in a state of beatitude or happiness.

2. Usage

The psalmists as well as the sages (there are eight beatitudes in Proverbs) appear particularly sensitive to the question of human happiness: "There are many who say, 'O that we might see some good!'" (4:6). They tried earnestly to find an answer to this fundamental question and to point the way toward greater human happiness. The twenty-six beatitudes in the Psalter are not magical formulas, nor are they recipes for happiness, but they do take the question seriously and endeavor to find some solution that can make happiness possible.

The word *ʾashrei* is the first word in the Psalter (and not only of Psalm 1), as if someone wanted to make it the gateway into the world of the psalms: "Happy are those/ who do not follow the advice of the wicked,/ . . . but their delight is in the law of the LORD" (1:1-2). To enter into this world one must be thirsting for happiness. The psalms bring good news for all the poor who seek happiness through all the circumstances of life, even the most difficult and tragic, all of which are evoked in the Psalter.

The concept of beatitude is generally meant to be more secular than blessedness. It has been said with justification that it represents the horizontal kind of happiness, as opposed to the vertical, and considers it more from the standpoint of those who enjoy it ("Happy are those") rather than the source ("Blessed be God"). It is true that this divine dimension is present in the Psalter ("You shall eat the fruit of the labor of your hands;/ you shall be happy, and it shall go well with you," 128:2; "Happy are those who observe justice,/ who do righteousness at all times," 106:3). But we see that such happiness in the Psalter is defined in terms of closeness to God: "Happy are those who take refuge in him" (34:8); "Happy are those who make the LORD their trust" (40:4); "Happy are those who consider the poor;/ the LORD delivers them in the day of trouble" (41:1); "Happy are those who live in your house. . . ./ Happy are those whose strength is in you" (84:4-5).

The happiness promised in the Psalter is not a private, individual affair; it is of necessity a communal enterprise: "Happy is the nation whose God is the LORD,/ the people whom he has chosen as his heritage" (33:12; see also 144:15).

HEART

LEV, LEVAV לב

Lev, Levav	
Total OT	853
1. Ps	137
2. Prov	99
3. Jer	66
Other Forms	2

1. Root

The two words *lev* and *levav* are used in the Bible to designate the heart. The word is derived from the root *lavav*, which means, depending on its conjugation, "to be deprived of understanding" (Song 4:9) or "to acquire understanding" (Job 11:12). Expressions such as "without heart" (Prov 9:4, 16; Jer 5:21) or "take to heart" (Exod 7:23; 9:21; 1 Sam 4:20) have nothing to do with affect, but address intelligence or understanding. The heart and wisdom, moreover, are often synonyms (1 Kgs 3:9ff.; Prov 10:8; 16:21; Job 9:4; 37:24).

2. Usage

The heart is, first of all, a physical organ, beating with the rhythm of life. In times of strong emotion, the heartbeat changes dramatically: "I am utterly spent and crushed;/ I groan because of the tumult of my heart" (38:8); "My heart throbs, my strength fails me" (38:10; see also 22:14; 37:15).

The psalmists and the other biblical authors go beyond the purely physical aspect of the heart to designate the interior mystery of the person. The heart is the center of the person, and it is in the heart that thoughts, intentions, decisions, feelings, and speech all take form. Senseless thoughts and speech also arise in the heart: "They think in their heart, 'We shall not be moved'" (10:6); "They think in their heart, 'God has forgotten'" (10:11). It is also in the heart that the just experience the presence of God, who knows him or her profoundly and gives support throughout life: "If you try my heart, if you visit me by night" (17:3); "You who test the minds and hearts,/ O righteous God" (7:9; see also 26:2; 44:22).

The heart appears as the seat of the emotions, as of fear, felt or resisted: "My heart is in anguish within me,/ the terrors of death have fallen upon me" (55:4); "Though an army encamp against me,/ my heart shall not fear" (27:3). It is the seat of anguish too, threatening from all sides: "Relieve the troubles of my heart/ and bring me out of my distress" (27:17). But the heart is also the seat of trust: "Wait for the LORD;/ be strong, and let your heart take courage" (27:14).

The heart can be invaded with sadness: "How long must I bear pain in my soul,/ and have sorrow in my heart all day long?" (13:2). But the psalmists clearly emphasize the heart as the seat of joyful emotions: "You have put gladness in my heart/ more than when their grain and wine abound" (4:7; see also 13:6; 104:15).

Finally, the heart plays the role of the creative will that conceives and undertakes its designs: "May he grant you your heart's desire,/ and fulfill all your plans" (20:4). Justice in works and speech can only come from the upright heart (7:10; 11:2; 32:11; 36:11; 64:11; 94:15; 97:11).

We should note also that in the Psalter, as everywhere in biblical anthropology, there is a close connection between the heart and the eyes (19:9; 101:5; 131:1). A person's eyes and look betray what is in his or her heart: thoughts of pride or of violence, or, on the contrary, of humility and compassion. To raise one's eyes toward the Lord is to hold one's heart and all one's life ready to serve the Lord: "To you I lift up my eyes,/ O you who are enthroned in the heavens!" (123:1).

HELP
(COME TO ONE'S HELP)

ʿAZAR עזר

ʿAzar	
Total OT	128
1. Ps	42
2. Isa	17
3. 2 Chr	15

1. Root

The 128 total occurrences include the verb (81x.) and two nouns derived from it, ʿezer (23x.) and ʿezrah (26x.). The root often has a military connotation; it denotes help in battle (Josh 1:14; 10:4, 6, 33; Judg 5:23; 2 Sam 8:5). The prophets were quick to point out the illusory character of the help expected from alliances with neighboring peoples, when Israel could have relied on help from Yahweh (Isa 20:6; 30:5; 31:1).

The concept of help also connotes the idea of common participation: the intervention of the one who comes to help is added to the efforts of the person or group who is helped (see also Josh 10:4ff.); the two ally themselves to accomplish a common task. The same meaning lies behind the help that woman brings to man (Gen 2:18, 20).

The help that the faithful hope for is above all divine help. We have some thirty uses of the verb with God as the subject, and there are many proper names derived from this root that are compounds with the divine name: Azariah, Eliezer, Eleazar, Lazarus, and Azriel.

2. Usage

It is immediately apparent that the help sought from God takes on a tone of urgency in the psalms. It is help that is needed right away, rather than ongoing, planned help, prepared ahead of time and spread out over an extended period. "But you, O LORD, do not be far away!/ O my help, come quickly to my aid!" (22:19; see also 38:22; 40:13; 70:1, 5; 71:12). There is no time to make plans or discuss the kinds of help to be brought. One thing is clear: God must intervene as quickly as possible: "You are my help and my deliverer;/ do not delay, O my God" (40:17).

In many instances, disappointment about help expected from other humans contributes to the sense of helplessness: "Trouble is near / and there is no one to help" (22:11), and again "O grant us help against the foe, / for human help is worthless" (108:12). We must therefore turn to the only reliable source of help: "My help comes from the LORD, / who made heaven and earth" (121:2).

Less often, but with considerable conviction, the word is used to refer to daily help, where God benevolently accompanies the faithful through all the happy and peaceful times, as well as during periods of distress and crisis: "Indeed you note trouble and grief, / . . . the helpless commit themselves to you; / you have been the helper of the orphan" (10:14); "May he send you help from the sanctuary, / and give you support" (20:2); "Let me live that I may praise you, / and let your ordinances help me" (119:175).

The assurance of divine help that is either recalled or hoped for is deeply rooted in the faith of Israel: "God is our refuge and strength, / a very present help in trouble" (46:1); "O Israel, trust in the LORD! / He is their help and their shield" (115:9). There is no greater happiness than to be able to count on God's help: "Happy are those whose help is the God of Jacob" (146:5).

HOLINESS

QODESH   קדש

Qodesh	
Total OT	842
1. Lev	152
2. Ezek	105
3. Exod	102
6. Ps	65

1. Root

The verb form of the root *qadash* (to be holy or to sanctify) is not found in the Psalter. The noun *qodesh* (holiness), however, is used frequently in the psalms (45x.), as is the adjective *qadosh* (holy; 15x.). The form *miqdash* is also found, applied to the Temple (5x.).

From the end of the last century until very recently the sense of sacredness in the Bible was universally thought to correspond to the notion of sacredness in other religions, including aspects of both fascination and terror. It was thought that the root *qadash,* used by the authors of the Bible to represent the sacred, necessarily implied the notion of separateness. This view is no longer universally held, and it does not entirely stand up to a close examination of the West-Semitic antecedents and the biblical texts, as has been shown by C. B. Costecalde.[1] For Costecalde, the root translates the notion of consecration and belonging. Still, respect for the text and for the uses of the root in the Psalter should perhaps induce us to retain the basic meaning of transcendence.

2. Usage

According to the psalms, the holiness of God is an inherent aspect of God's mystery: the divine name is holy (33:21; 103:1; 105:3; 106:47; 111:9; 145:21), and proclaiming the holiness of God is an integral part of Israel's faith. "Yet you are holy,/ enthroned on the praises of Israel" (22:3; see also 30:5; 99:3, 5, 9). The thesis that the holiness of God emphasized God's transcendence is supported by the fact that this attribute is found most often in the context of the kingship of Yahweh (47:9; 93:5; 96:9; 97:12; 98:1; 99:5, 9). It is also remarkable that we find in this same context of holiness the epithets great and awesome, and the attributes of power and glory: "Your people will offer themselves willingly/ on the day you lead your forces/ on the holy mountains" (110:3); "Holy and awesome is his name" (111:9; see also 29:2; 63:3; 77:14; 89:6-8).

Holiness in the Psalter is also applied to places: the holy mountain, especially Zion (2:6; 3:5; 15:1; 43:3; 48:2; 87:1), but also Sinai (68:18), the holy temple (5:8; 11:4; 65:5; 79:1; 138:2), the holy place (24:2), the Holy of Holies (28:2), the holy throne (47:9), the holy realm (78:54), the holy dwelling (68:6), the high places, God's sanctuary (102:20). These are precisely those places where God is encountered and where one desires to live: "O LORD, who may abide in your tent?/ Who may dwell on your holy hill?" (15:1; see also 24:3); "O send out your light and your truth;/ let them lead me;/ let them bring me to your holy hill/ and to your dwelling" (43:3).

Nowhere in the psalms do we find the idea of the holiness of a human being as an ideal of personal perfection to strive for. In the few instances where a human being is said to be holy, what is emphasized is the belongingness that exists between an individual or a group and the God of holiness.

1. Originally in *Dictionnaire de la Bible. Supplément* X (1985) cols. 1346–94, then in his book, *Aux origines du sacré biblique* (Paris: Letouzey & Ané, 1986) 156.

HUMAN (BEING)

>ADAM   אדם

>Adam	
Total OT	554
1. Ezek	132
2. Ps	62
3. Eccl	49
Other Forms	225

1. Root

The Psalter uses three generic words for the human being: *>adam* (43x.), *>ish* (43x.—fem.: *>ishah;* 2x.), and *>enosh* (13x.). The first is the most frequently used. It means the earthly one, one who comes from the earth and belongs to the earth. The second term signifies a relationship, usually to *>ishah*, the woman, used very seldom in the psalms. Back in the times before feminism, the words *>adam* and *>ish* were generic and used for both genders. The last word, *>enosh*, emphasizes the mortal nature of the human being.

2. Usage

The psalms bring out the paradoxical nature of the human being who, on the one hand, is called to a kingly role, and, on the other hand, is fragile in the extreme.

The kingly vocation of human beings appears clearly in the well-known verses of Psalm 8: "When I look at your heavens,/

the work of your fingers,/ the moon and the stars that you have established;/ what are human beings that you are mindful of them,/ mortals that you care for them?/ Yet you have made them a little lower than God,/ and crowned them with glory and honor" (vv. 3-5). Those who are infinitely small in the vast universe are placed at the summit of creation. And in just as striking terms, Psalm 115 emphasizes the immensity of the domain given to humanity to govern: "The heavens are the LORD's heavens,/ but the earth he has given to human beings" (115:16). Working in concert with God, humans finish the work of his creation with their daily labor (104:14, 23).

But the sense of human fragility is even more acute in the Psalter, where we find some of the vocabulary and preoccupations of Ecclesiastes: "You have made my days a few handbreadths,/ and my lifetime is as nothing in your sight./ Surely everyone stands as a mere breath./ Surely everyone goes about like a shadow" (39:5-6; see also 62:10; 94:11; 144:3). The human being is seen as fodder for death: "You turn us [*'enosh*—in the third person Hebrew] back to dust,/ and say, 'Turn back, you mortals'" (90:3; see also 89:48).

Judgment is sometimes even more severe, to the point of unjustly finding nothing at all good in humanity: "The LORD looks down from heaven on humankind/ to see if there are any who are wise,/ who seek after God./ They have all gone astray, they are all alike perverse;/ there is no one who does good,/ no, not one" (14:2-3; see also 53:3). But we must not take this as definitive truth. This is an exceptional emergency, when the excess of evil leads to such generalizations, which are intended more to shake up the apathy and complacency of the majority of people and lead to their conversion.

Between the two extremes of the paradox, kingly vocation and human fragility, there is a wider reality that reveals God as favoring human happiness: "Come and see what God has done:/ he is awesome in his deeds among mortals" (66:5; see also 84:6; 107:8, 15, 21, 31). We find, then, that the Good News of God's love for humanity is written deep in the heart of the Old Testament (see Luke 2:14; John 3:16). Humanity is the locus for the evangelization of the world: "They shall speak of the glory of your kingdom . . ./ to make known to all people your mighty deeds" (145:11-12).

Are the Psalms a Masculine Prayer?

The lives of women hold little place in the psalms. This is not surprising in a Scripture produced by a religion and a society where women had little status and no official recognition of their institutions. This can only be regretted. While it is true that women can find themselves in the universality of much of the prayer of the psalms, it is nevertheless indisputable that their lives and their particular human experience are given scant attention in the psalms.

To start with, there are the absences or silences: not one psalm is attributed to a woman, contrary to other biblical songs, such as the canticles of Miriam, Deborah, Hannah, Judith, Esther, etc.

Not one woman is mentioned by name in the psalms, except Bathsheba, whose mention remains somewhat indirect (51:1). The experience of faith of women such as Sarah, Hagar, Rachel, Miriam, and others is left out of the commemorations of the Psalter, where Moses, Aaron, Samuel, David, and others are remembered.

The term ʾishah (woman) is only used twice (109:9 and 128:3), and even then indirectly; the word is never found in the plural, which further leaves the collective experience of women in the shadows.

This being so, what can be said about the references to women that do appear in the Psalter? There are about twenty-six such references, and always about a certain type of woman: a young girl, a wife, a mother, a servant woman, a widow.

The figure of the widow appears five times. One of these verses, scarcely edifying, is a curse (109:9);

the other four are references to types of persons in society who are in need of divine protection (68:6; 78:64; 94:6; 146:9).

The reference to the mother, the breast, or the mother's womb is classic language that stands for the moment of birth and man's appearance in the world (22:10-11; 51:7; 71:6; 131:2; 139:13). The expression "son of your servant woman" (86:16; 116:16) is used to signify the human condition, and perhaps a state of belonging to God in faith.

Psalm 45 contains the most material that speaks of the life and destiny of a woman; it celebrates the beauty and glory of the king's daughter. A few psalms mention young girls taking part in liturgical celebrations and wedding or royal processions (45:15; 68:26; 78:63; 148:12).

There are two instances where feelings are compared to those felt by or about women: "I went about as one who laments for a mother,/ bowed down and in mourning" (35:14); and, "Trembling took hold of them there,/ pains as of a woman in labor" (48:6).

In summary, even if we attribute these silences concerning the lives of women to cultural differences, it is certain that, given today's mentality, it behooves us to transcend these limitations and breathe new life into the prayer of the psalms by bringing into them the viewpoint of women.

(THE) JUST

TSADDIQ צדיק

Tsadaq	
Total OT	523
1. Ps	139
2. Prov	94
3. Isa	81

1. Root

The 139 uses of the root *tsadaq* include the verb (4x.), the adjective *tsaddiq* (52x.), and the two nouns *tsedeq* (49x.) and *tsedaqah* (34x.). This last word is used in the majority of instances referring to a person's relationship to God and in parallel with or as a synonym to *teshuʿah* (salvation). It would thus mean the saving justice of God. *Tsedeq* is also used of God, but is more commonly found referring to humans. It has three main meanings: the objective right of persons, the respect of this right (social justice), and the quality of relationship with God—one is *tsaddiq* if he or she respects God's plans for the world. This adjective, then, describes someone who observes God's commands. For this reason it is one of the principal designations of the believer in the Psalter.

2. Usage

The psalmists emphasize the justice of God: "Establish the righteous,/ you who test the minds and hearts,/ O righteous God" (7:9); "God is a righteous judge" (7:11); "The LORD is just in all his ways" (145:17). But what is the justice of God? Most often, as in the last quotation, this justice is the order that God has put into the world. We could say that the justice of God has a cosmological dimension.

The second dimension is *salvific*. God's justice is not a justice of trials and courts, but one of salvation and liberation: "The LORD works vindication/ and justice for all who are oppressed" (103:6). It is not a justice that condemns and overwhelms, but one that inspires and edifies; not a justice that one fears, but a justice that one hopes for. There is no dilemma in the Bible in general or in the psalms in particular between justice and mercy; the justice of God *is* mercy: "He loves righteousness and justice;/ the earth is full of the steadfast love of the LORD" (33:5).

31

Finally, the psalms of the kingship of Yahweh open up the perspective of a final judgment: "He is coming to judge the earth./ He will judge the world with righteousness,/ and the peoples with his truth" (96:13); "He is coming to judge the earth./ He will judge the world with righteousness,/ and the peoples with equity" (98:9).

Human justice, on the other hand, seems at first sight to be synonymous with social justice. Only those "who walk blamelessly, and do what is right" (15:2) will be able to dwell on the holy mountain. This justice manifests itself in truthful speech, respect for one's kin and one's neighbor, faithfulness to one's word once given, and disinterested financial help to those in need (Psalm 15). Psalm 112 sings the praises of the just person and describes the felicity of the upright (v. 4); "It is well with those who deal generously and lend,/ who conduct their affairs with justice" (112:5); "They have distributed freely, they have given to the poor;/ their righteousness endures forever" (112:9).

Such justice is also the religious attitude of the person who is conscious of living in a state of truth with God. To be just is to understand and live out the demands of the covenant, to live in harmony with the world of God, with the way God wants us to see and act: "Let the righteous rejoice in the LORD/ and take refuge in him./ Let all the upright in heart glory" (64:10).

Those Problematical "Enemies"

The Psalter expresses wonderfully the hope and faith of Israel, reflecting a profound consciousness of the love that binds the faithful to God, as well as the justice that is expected of them in dealing with their neighbor and the poor. But there is a shadow in the picture: the comportment of the Israel of the Bible toward those who were considered the enemy. It is somewhat shocking—even scandalous—to find in a book of prayers that express all the essence of the faith of a people the constant attention paid to the existence of the enemy and the punishment meted out to them.

There is no getting away from the fact that the enemy is omnipresent in the psalms. Even if we limit ourselves to the three most common names given to the enemy, there are a total of 153 references to them. These three names are *ᵓoyeb* (enemy; 74x.), *tzorer* (adversary; 47x.), and *soneᵓ* (the one who hates; 32x.). That is an impressive number! The question is, is it too much? We might say that, for one thing, the psalms describe a world of profound divisions among peoples, who come to regard each other as enemies.

And it is also a fact that the Israel of the Bible was a tiny power, often the pawn of super-powers, and suffered enormously from constant invasions and occupations at the hands of "enemy" nations. However, the very notion of enemy is one of mutual relating: if Israel speaks so often of its enemies, might it not do well to honestly confront its own attitudes? Can Israel itself pretend total innocence? Can it claim that it has never *made* an enemy?

What we find even more shocking, perhaps, is the intransigence we find even in prayer toward the enemy: "I pursued my enemies and overtook them;/ and did not turn back until they were consumed./ I struck them down, so that they were not able to rise" (18:37-38). It seems shocking to read the following in the same prayer that speaks of the certitude of being surrounded by the loving presence of God: "Do I not hate those who hate you, O LORD?/ And do I not loathe those who rise up against you?" (139:21). Even if we acknowledge that Semitic languages are not given to euphemisms, and that hatred here may simply mean justified indignation, that does not do much to mitigate what seems truly excessive in the feelings expressed here.

So what can we say today about this problem? First of all, there *are* enemies in the world; there are wars. Conflicts and quarrels between nations, groups, and individuals remind us that human relations are still often embroiled in hostility. Second, we are or we can be enemies of others. The fault is not always on the other side, and we would do well to ask ourselves some hard questions about our own responsibility in fostering conflict. And third, we must remember the evangelical precept of forgiveness of one's enemies. Such an attitude is the only way to break out of this vicious circle of hatred: "Love your enemies and pray for those who persecute you, so that you may be children of your Father in heaven" (Matt 5:44-45).

KING

MELEK מֶלֶךְ

Melek	
Total OT	3,154
1. 2 Kgs	466
2. 2 Chr	396
3. 1 Kgs	391
11. Ps	86

1. Root

After *ben* (son) and *ʾelohim* (God), *melek* (king) is the third most frequently used noun in the Bible (2,526 occurrences). The root is well known in all the ancient Semitic languages, and its meaning is clear: be king, rule. The root occurs eighty-six times in the Psalter, with the verb "to rule" appearing six times (always with God as the subject), the noun "king" *(melek)* sixty-seven times, and the feminine nouns for "kingdom" and "domain" thirteen times.

2. Usage

Prayers on behalf of the king help us understand what it was that the people expected from him. In wartime, they wanted only one thing—victory: "Give victory to the king, O LORD" (20:9; see also 18:51; 21:2). In peacetime God's task was even more formidable, since God had to ensure that justice was carried out and that the poor and helpless were not oppressed: "Give the king your justice, O God,/ and your righteousness to a king's son./ May he judge your people with righteousness,/ and your poor with justice" (72:1-2).

But true royalty is something else again. The refrain "The Lord is king" reminds us how relative the earthly kingship of men is (47:9; 93:1; 96:10; 97:1; 99:1). The kingship of God goes back to the beginnings of creation. "The Lord is king" simply because he created all things by his victory over primitive chaos: "The LORD is king. . . ./ He has established the world; it shall never be moved" (93:1; see also 96:10). He is king because he ever holds sway over all the cosmic forces: "The LORD sits enthroned over the flood;/ the LORD sits enthroned as king forever" (29:10). For these reasons, his kingship is universal: "Clap your hands, all you peoples;/ . . . for the LORD, the Most High, is awesome,/ a great king over all the earth" (47:1-2; see also 98:6).

Moreover, Israel has witnessed historical manifestations of God's kingship. God is king, for Israel, because God has time and time again delivered the chosen people from their enemies: "You are my king and my God;/ you command victories for Jacob" (44:4); "For the LORD, the Most High, is awesome,/ a great king over all the earth./ He subdued peoples under us,/ and nations under our feet" (47:2-3). Of course, these claims are not without their ambiguity; but Israel, happily, has recognized that the kingship of God is other than that of earthly rulers, their own or those of neighboring peoples: "Righteousness and justice are the foundation of your throne;/ steadfast love and faithfulness go before you" (89:14); "Mighty king, lover of justice,/ you have established equity;/ you have executed justice and righteousness in Jacob" (99:4).

Finally, the kingship of God has an eschatological dimension, which will not prevail until the end of time: "Say among the nations, 'The LORD is king!/ . . . He will judge the peoples with equity.'/ . . . He will judge the world with righteousness,/ and the peoples with his truth" (96:10, 13); "He will judge the world with righteousness,/ and the peoples with equity" (98:9). Rivalries between nations will cease, and the kings of the earth will join in procession as one people of God, happy to celebrate the salvation offered to all the nations: "Because of your temple at Jerusalem/ kings bear gifts to you" (68:29; see also 72:10-11; 138:4).

LAW

TORAH   תורה

Torah	
Total OT	220
1. Ps	36
2. Deut	22
3. Neh	21
Other Forms	51

1. Root

Two principle explanations have been advanced for the etymology of the word *torah* (teaching, instruction), often translated as Law and deriving from the root *yarah*. According to the first theory, the verb means to point with the finger, point out a direction. Understood in this sense, *torah* would mean a practical guide, an orientation for our behavior in life. The second theory interprets the verb in the sense of throwing or shooting, as in throwing the dice, in order to obtain an oracle or an instruction. From this starting point, the verb would have come to mean instruct, teach (Exod 4:12, 15; 2 Kgs 12:3; Ps 119:102).

2. *Usage*

There are two striking features of the use of this word in the Psalter. The first is that *torah* is always personalized, so to speak, in that it is always mentioned in relation to God: the law of the Lord, your law, his law, the law of his God. Second, the word is used in concentration in Psalm 119, which contains twenty-five of the thirty-six total occurrences in the Psalter, representing the greatest frequency of the entire Old Testament.

If we accept the first etymology of the word—direction—then we understand clearly its use as way or path: "The law of their God is in their hearts;/ their steps do not slip" (37:31); "They did not keep God's covenant,/ but refused to walk according to his law" (78:10); "If his children forsake my law/ and do not walk according to my ordinances" (89:30); "Happy are those whose way is blameless,/ who walk in the law of the LORD" (119:1); "The arrogant utterly deride me,/ but I do not turn away from your law" (119:51). What we see here is not a collection of rules to observe, but a way of living to be followed, an orientation to live out. It implies the choice of a particular life.

As for the second etymology, the psalmists clearly express the meaning of *torah* as revelation. This is seen in Psalm 119, which speaks of the word at least twenty times, alternately with *torah*. One keeps the *torah* as one keeps the word; the primary role of *torah* is to shed light and to point out a direction: "Happy are those whom you discipline, O LORD,/ and whom you teach out of your law" (94:12); "Teach me, O LORD, the way of your statutes" (119:33).

When we speak of Law, we often think of an abstract code, an arid legal text, separate from life. But this was not so for the psalmists. For them, Law leads directly into life, and it is celebrated as something gratifying and a source of joy: "The law of the LORD is perfect,/ reviving the soul" (19:7). The long Psalm 119, with each stanza multiplying the synonyms of the word Law (ways, decrees, precepts, will, ordinances, statutes, etc.), lays special emphasis on the delights afforded by observance of the Law: "I delight in your law" (v. 70, see also vv. 77, 92, 174). Far from being felt as an obstacle to happiness, *torah* is longed for and lived out lovingly by the whole person: "I delight to do your will, O my God;/ your law is within my heart" (40:8).

LISTEN

SHAMA< שמע

Shama<	
Total OT	1,159
1. Jer	158
2. Deut	86
3. Isa	86
4. Ps	77
Other Forms	55

1. Root

The basic meaning of the verb *shama<* is to hear, to perceive a sound, a noise, a word. But it has been used to express a great variety of meanings: (1) to listen, to pay attention; (2) to obey; (3) to answer a prayer; (4) to understand; (5) to examine.

The faith of the Israelites rests first and foremost on the fact that they listen to and accept a word that has come from elsewhere: "Hear, O Israel: The LORD is our God, the LORD alone" (Deut 6:4). The author of Deuteronomy introduces the decalogue with the same verb: "Hear, O Israel, the statutes and ordinances that I am addressing to you today" (Deut 5:1). What comes first is not the carrying out of prescribed behaviors, humankind's effort to reach God, but rather our openness to the word and our receiving it in love. Faith, as Paul will say so well, is born from what is heard (*"fides ex auditu,"* Rom 10:17).

2. Usage

The place par excellence where the word is heard is among the people, the community, which keeps the memory of all the events of salvation that have occurred over its long history: "We have heard with our ears, O God,/ our ancestors have told us,/ what deeds you performed in their days,/ in the days of old" (44:1; see also 78:3-4).

But the same verb *shamaᶜ* is used to express the whole tragedy of Israel, rebellious and disobedient, often unable to keep the word that was received: "But my people did not listen to my voice;/ Israel would not submit to me" (81:11). And this tragedy of Israel becomes also the personal tragedy of God: "O that my people would listen to me,/ that Israel would walk in my ways" (81:13). God, however, never gives up hope that the chosen people will return, and again and again asks of them the same thing: "O that today you would listen to his voice!" (95:7).

The word is first proclaimed and received in the midst of the community, and then the individual listens to it even more attentively: "Once God has spoken;/ twice I have heard this" (62:11); "Let me hear what God the LORD will speak" (85:8). The whole of life for the believer can be summed up in the beautiful invocation of Psalm 143: "Let me hear of your steadfast love in the morning" (143:8).

Listening to the word remains a risky enterprise, a true challenge, necessitating many serious confrontations: "Hear, O my people, while I admonish you;/ O Israel, if you would but listen to me!/ There shall be no strange god among you" (81:8-9; see also 50:7).

The fact that the psalms express so many appeals and cries to God shows that their authors and those who prayed the psalms were convinced that God is above all the one who listens. And this conviction rests on *a fortiori* reasoning: "He who planted the ear, does he not hear?" (94:9). Daily experience has provided the evidence again and again: "O LORD, in the morning you hear my voice" (5:3; see also 6:9-10). The poor are privileged witnesses: "This poor soul cried, and was heard by the LORD" (34:6; see also 69:34).

LIVE

CHAYAH חיה

Chayah	
Total OT	777
1. Gen	125
2. Ezek	107
3. Ps	81

1. Root

The four most common forms of the root are the verb *chayah* (284x.), the adjective *chay* (alive; 236x.), the feminine singular noun *chayah* (living being; 97x.), and the masculine plural noun *chayim* (life; 148x.). The concept of life in the Old Testament primarily represents physical life, but it is used in such a way that it reflects great sensitivity to the quality of life of the human being and all that contributes to his or her well-being. Life is also seen as the reward for fidelity to the commandments and the Word of God.

2. Usage

The whole Psalter is full of a deep and invincible love of life: "Which of you desires life,/ and covets many days to enjoy good?" (34:12). Life is the supreme blessing, the gift that all desire above anything else: "He asked you for life; you gave it to him—/ length of days for ever and ever" (21:4).

For the psalmists, life means not only human life—whether individual life or that of the whole people—but also animal life and all of creation: "Let everything that breathes praise the LORD!" (150:6).

But such a profound appreciation of life does not mean that the psalmists do not deeply feel all the tragic aspects of existence. Life is never taken for granted, but is an unending struggle against evil, pain, suffering, and death: "For my life is spent with sorrow,/ and my years with sighing" (31:10); "For my soul is full of troubles,/ and my life draws near to Sheol" (88:3). The psalmists see beyond the life of the individual, too, and speak of that inescapable reality that all face one day: death. Like Qoheleth (Ecclesiastes) after them, the psalmists invite us to reflect upon this mystery of life that inescapably leads to death: "Truly, no ransom avails for one's life,/ there is no price one can give to God for it./ For the ransom of life is costly,/ and can never suffice/ that one should live on forever/ and never see the grave" (49:7-9). Death remains the ultimate obstacle, and the psalmists implore God to save them from it.

But even when facing death in all its forms, they nevertheless do not lose their total faith in the God of life and all the living, sure that he will save them yet. Even the last obstacle can be overcome: "O LORD, you brought up my soul from Sheol,/ restored me to life from among those gone down to the Pit" (30:3); "Truly the eye of the LORD is on those who fear him,/ on those who hope in his steadfast love,/ to deliver their soul from death,/ and to keep them alive in famine" (33:18-19); "For you have delivered my soul from death,/ and my feet from falling,/ so that I may walk before God in the light of life" (56:13).

The God of the psalms is not the abstract deity of the philosophers, but the living God who is close to his creatures, full of love, and giving life: "My soul thirsts for God, for the living God" (42:2); "My soul longs, indeed it faints/ for the courts of the LORD;/ my heart and my flesh sing for joy/ to the living God" (84:2). It is to this God of life that we turn to find strength and taste for life, as in this cry that occurs again and again as a pattern in Psalm 119: "Give me life!" (vv. 25, 37, 40, 88, 107, 149, 154, 156, 159).

LOVE

CHESED   חסד

Chesed	
Total OT	245
1. Ps	127
2. 2 Sam	12
3. Prov	10
Other Forms	3

1. Root

The word *chesed* is of uncertain etymology and is unknown in the other ancient Semitic languages. The corresponding verb is only used three times in the Bible (2 Sam 22:26; Ps 18:26; Prov 5:10) and the adjective *chasid,* faithful, appears thirty-two times, twenty-five of which appear in the Psalter. The ancient translations (the Septuagint and the Vulgate) generally interpreted *chesed* in the sense of mercy, translating with, respectively, the words *eleos* and *misericordia.*

However, recent research has refined our understanding of the word. *Chesed* belongs to the language of covenant and the relationship of covenanted parties. It defines and qualifies these mutual relationships. Its fundamental meaning is loyalty and faithfulness to a covenant. Nevertheless, the term does have a variety of other meanings, as we see from our modern translations: love (used frequently in the liturgy), grace, goodness, lovingkindness. These translations emphasize the emotional aspect, the interior disposition of the *chesed;* however, we must not lose sight of the concrete meaning of the term as the act of faithfulness to a covenant that derives from a situation of solidarity between the one who is faithful and the recipient of the faithfulness (Gen 24:12, 14; 2 Sam 2:6; 9:7; 15:20; Ps 18:51).

2. *Usage*

Except for a few rare exceptions (Ps 109:12, 16; 141:5), which speak of human *chesed,* the psalms enthusiastically celebrate the *chesed* of God. A familiar refrain— "for his steadfast love endures forever" (106:1; see also 118:1-4; 136:1-26)—makes God's *chesed* the primary characteristic of the God of the covenant and thus reproduces one of the major elements of the revelation received by Moses (Exod 34:6) of a God "merciful and gracious,/ slow to anger and abounding in steadfast love and faithfulness" (Ps 86:15; see also 103:8; 145:8). The *chesed* that is hoped for in human relationships is found in incomparably greater plenitude in God. The God of the psalmists is essentially a faithful God, who can be counted upon at all times and in any situation.

Two other qualities complete the description of divine *chesed:* mercy (or lovingkindness) and truthfulness. The first is associated with God eight times in the psalms: "Be mindful of your mercy, O LORD, and of your steadfast love" (25:6); "Have mercy on me, O God,/ according to your steadfast love;/ according to your abundant mercy/ blot out my transgressions" (51:1; see also 40:11; 69:16; 86:15; 103:4, 8; 145:8). The second quality, truthfulness, is even more often attributed to God—some fifteen times (see 25:10; 26:3; 40:11-12).

The component of reciprocity, present everywhere in the biblical use of the word, is clear as well from the usage of the derived adjective, *chasid,* a term that can designate either the source of the *chesed* or the beneficiary. The *chasid* tries to be faithful to God, but has already experienced God's faithfulness toward him- or herself. This situation lies behind the ambiguity—perhaps intentional—of the phrase "the love of God": it can mean the love the faithful one bears for God, just as well as the love of God toward the faithful, a love that gives his or her existence all its meaning.

PEACE

SHALOM שלום

Shalom	
Total OT	237
1. Jer	31
2. Isa	29
3. Ps	27
Other Forms 237	

1. Root

Shalom is certainly one of the best-known Hebrew words, even to those with no knowledge of Semitic languages. In modern times the word is used by Jews as an everyday formula of greeting, the equivalent of hello and goodbye (see salutations in the Bible in Judg 19:20; 1 Sam 25:6; 2 Kgs 4:23, 26).

The word and its derivatives are well known and confirmed in the ancient Semitic languages, with the meanings peace and friendship. It belongs to the root *shalem,* which means to be healthy, whole, complete. Peace, then, is a sensation of plenitude, of achievement and harmony, grounded in the integrated well-being of the whole person or entire nation. The opposite is war (as it is in our modern languages) and every-thing connected with fighting—quarrels, fights, plots, weapons, etc. Such vocabulary holds an astonishingly large place in the Bible.

2. *Usage*

Peace can be an individual matter. In this case, it is to be understood as health or safety. It is first a feeling of well-being, physical and emotional health, experienced as a blessing of God: "Great is the LORD,/ who delights in the welfare [peace] of his servant" (35:27). It can refer also to an emotional state that allows us to overcome and alleviate a feeling of anguish, at times crushing and unbearable: "There is no soundness in my flesh/ because of your indignation;/ there is no health [peace] in my bones because of my sin" (38:3). Freed from this state of anguish, the psalmist bears witness to the deep peace that has come upon him: "I will both lie down and sleep in peace;/ for you alone, O LORD, make me lie down in safety" (4:8).

There is also social peace. This peace is yet to be achieved, given the number of quarrels, conflicts, and fights that in-evitably are a part of life: "I am for peace;/ but when I speak,/ they are for war" (120:7); "He will redeem me unharmed/ from the battle that I wage,/ for many are arrayed against me" (55:18).

There is also the peace that people talk of, without really wanting it (28:3; 35:20). It is a deceptive word, a slogan used by people who are hatching evil plots: "Too long have I had my dwelling/ among those who hate peace" (120:6). Fortu-nately, it is more than just a word for other people, and for these it is a goal dear to their hearts, which they pray for. For them, it is a peace ardently desired out of love for their brethren: "Pray for the peace of Jerusalem:/ 'May they prosper who love you'/ For the sake of my relatives and friends/ I will say, 'Peace be within you'" (122:6, 8).

Israel often experienced the utter devastation of war, and when the Israelites returned from Exile the peace that had seemed unattainable was seen as the most precious of the gifts of God: "He grants peace within your borders" (147:14). From now on Israel can dream of a new and definitive peace:

"Faithfulness will spring up from the ground,/ and righteousness will look down from the sky" (85:11).

PEOPLE

ʿAM   עַם

ʿAm	
Total OT	1,868
1. Exod	175
2. Jer	165
3. Isa	130
4. Ps	120

1. Root

Even though biblical Hebrew has not kept the verb form of this root, ʿam derives from a well-known Semitic root ʿamam, which means to include. There are two other words meaning people in the Psalter: goy (used 60x.), and leʾom (used 14x.). All three stand for the same thing, but goy (plural: goyim) was usually reserved for foreign peoples, considered pagan, whereas ʿam emphasized the sense of belonging to a family, a clan, or a people. It was the latter, then, that was used more often to stand for Israel, the people of God.

2. Usage

The usage of the word ʿam points out the obvious tension in the thought of Israel between its specialness and the universality of its vocation.

A theme throughout Exodus, Numbers, Deuteronomy, Jeremiah, and the book of Psalms is the privileged relationship Israel enjoyed with God, a relationship based on a completely free choice on God's part, as well as a whole series of divine interventions in favor of Israel. The people's happiness is the result of this state of divine election: "Happy is the nation whose God is the LORD,/ the people whom he has chosen as his heritage" (33:12). Israel is God's inheritance (28:9; 94:14; 106:40), the flock of God the shepherd (77:21; 78:52). The psalms are strewn with confessions of faith, acknowledging that the people belong to God: "Know that the LORD is God./ It is he that made us, and we are his;/ we are his people, and the sheep of his pasture" (100:3); "For his is our God,/ and we are the people of his pasture,/ and the sheep of his hand" (95:7).

We hear also of the signal events of the epic of Exodus, which is above all the story of the powerful and marvelous interventions of God on Israel's behalf: "So he brought his people out with joy" (105:43); "[He] who led his people through the wilderness,/ for his steadfast love endures forever" (136:16). But the psalmists are well aware that the great adventure of Exodus sometimes took on the aspect of a trying ordeal, marked by the frequent rebellions of "this stiff-necked people": "But my people did not listen to my voice;/ Israel would not submit to me" (81:11); "For forty years I loathed that generation/ and said, 'They are a people whose hearts go astray,/ and they do not regard my ways'" (95:10). In a number of places the psalms state that the Lord is actually pursuing a lawsuit against the people: "He calls to the heavens above/ and to the earth, that he may judge his people" (50:4; see also 72:2; 135:14).

The special vocation of the people of Israel does not isolate them from the other nations, but makes them witnesses sent to the nations. The people of the Lord anxiously await the day when all the nations of the earth will join in the praise and glorification of God: "Clap your hands, all you peoples;/ shout to God with loud songs of joy" (47:1); "Bless our God, O peoples,/ let the sound of his praise be heard" (66:8); "Let the nations be glad and sing for joy./ . . . Let the peoples praise you, O God;/ let all the peoples praise you" (67:4-5).

The Our Father, the Perfect Psalm

Jesus prayed the psalms and was deeply influenced by their theology and spirituality. It is noticeable that the great majority of quotations from the Psalter found in the New Testament are recited by Jesus, and most of them during the most critical period of his life: his death and resurrection (see M. Gourgues, *Les psaumes et Jésus — Jésus et les psaumes* [Paris: Cerf, 1978] 62). Identifying himself with the poor and the *tsaddiq* (the just man) who cries out from his suffering in the psalms, Jesus takes on all the cries for help of suffering humanity, as well as the fight for the triumph of life over death.

The Our Father does not contain any actual quotations from the psalms, but every phrase, every word harks back to them, with the exception of the precept about forgiving one's debtors. In Psalm 145 alone we find a number of elements found in the Our Father:

—the sanctification of the name: "I will extol you, my God and King,/ and bless your name for ever and ever" (145:1; see also vv. 2, 21);

—the coming of the Kingdom: "They shall speak of the glory of your kingdom. . . ./ Your kingdom is an everlasting kingdom" (145:11, 13);

—the giving of the daily bread: "The eyes of all look to you,/ and you give them their food in due season./ You open your hand,/ satisfying the desire of every living thing" (145:15-16);

—help against temptation: "The LORD upholds all who are falling,/ and raises up all who are bowed down" (145:14).

The God of the Our Father is the God of the Psalter, a God infinitely great yet infinitely close, holy and kingly, who gives, pardons, and delivers from evil.

The Our Father, like the psalms, expresses two particular cries of the human heart: the one, a prayer of praise ("hallowed be thy name"); the other, a cry for help, a supplication.

The two poles of human happiness (Psalm 1) and the glory of God (Psalm 150) are also found in the Our Father, although in the opposite order: the Our Father opens with the glory of God and ends with what leads to human happiness. But these two poles are not really opposites, because everything is to be accomplished "on earth as it is in heaven."

There are two things that are new in the Our Father and are not found in the psalms. One is the absolute confidence with which Christians address God as father—this occurs in the psalms, but not as the usual way to pray to God. Here the name father replaces the old name of Yahweh and becomes normative in Christian prayer. The other new element is the insistence upon our forgiving those who have hurt us. The psalms often speak of the forgiveness we hope for from God, but never of that forgiveness that we are to show our brethren. On this point the Our Father introduces something radically new.

PITY

RACHAMIM רחמים

Rachamim	
Total OT	131
1. Ps	25
2. Isa	17
3. Jer	17

1. Root

The idea of pity or tenderness is conveyed in Hebrew by the root *racham*, which evokes the maternal womb *(rechem)* and consequently the inner impulses and feelings of tenderness of a woman. The very word brings to mind a certain image, recalling the love and affection that a mother shows her child. By applying it to God as the principle subject of the verb and the unique subject of the verbal adjective *rachum* (merciful, except for 112:4), the Bible is implicitly saying that God has a mother's visage.

2. Usage

Psalm 110 contains a metaphor applied to the birth of the Messiah that enables us to get a feeling for the original, concrete meaning of the word *rechem:* "From the womb of the morning,/ like dew, your youth will come to you" (110:3).

The pity of God is not just one more attribute, among a whole list of others, that was recognized only later on, or only on certain occasions during Israel's history. From the time of the revelation on Mount Sinai the pity of the God of the covenant was seen as God's most fundamental attribute, the principle emblem of God's love: "But you, O Lord, are a God merciful and gracious,/ slow to anger and abounding in steadfast love and faithfulness" (86:15; see also 103:8; 111:4; 116:5; 145:8, 9). God's very essence is pity, and Israel had first-hand experience of God's pity throughout its history, a history marked by sin, as God again and again granted life-giving pardon: "Answer me, O LORD, for your steadfast love is good;/ according to your abundant mercy, turn to me" (69:16); "Yet he, being compassionate,/ forgave their iniquity,/ and did not destroy them" (78:38); "Great is your mercy, O LORD" (119:156). Israel may not have always been entirely confident when facing the God of mercy, but its cries and supplications were no less sincere and heartrending: "Has God forgotten to be gracious?/ Has he in anger shut up his compassion?" (77:9); "Do not remember against us the iniquities of our ancestors;/ let your compassion come speedily to meet us" (79:8; see also 102:14).

Given that compassion is an attribute almost exclusively reserved to God, the few places where the root *racham* is applied to humans are all the more forceful. There are, in fact, only three occurrences in the Psalter of this word being used in reference to humans. The first such instance is undoubtedly unique in the Bible as a whole: "I love you, O LORD, my strength" (18:1). In Hebrew, the verb is in the future tense and is introduced by the set phrase "and he said." It is actually a statement of intention, a purpose decided upon that is in reality a response to a loving initiative on the part of the Lord: "He delivered me, because he delighted *[hafets]* in me" (18:19; see also v. 51).

The second occurrence is particularly interesting because of the comparison that it draws between divine love and human love: "As a father has compassion for his children,/ so the LORD has compassion for those who fear him" (103:13). This already tells us something about the nature of God's love for us.

Finally, the third place where this word is used of humans is in the description of the just person: "They rise in the darkness as a light for the upright;/ they are gracious, merciful, and righteous" (112:4). This call to brotherly forbearance is all the more welcome because it is rare (along with Prov 10:12 and Wis 12:22) in departing from the more "natural" vengeance and violence invoked upon the enemy elsewhere in the psalms.

POOR

ʿANI   עני

ʿAni	
Total OT	219
1. Ps	67
2. Isa	23
3. Job	15

1. Root

Derived from the root ʿanah, which means (in the intensive conjugation) oppress, do violence to, subjugate, the three nouns ʿanaw, ʿani (poor), and ʿoni (poverty) describe more an objective situation than an interior, subjective one. Since it means more a state of poverty that is inflicted from the outside rather than a poverty that is chosen, humiliated, rather than humble, would be a closer translation of the Hebrew. The vocabulary of poverty in the psalms includes two other synonymous adjectives: ʾebyon (23x.) and rash (once).

2. Usage

The poor are, above all, those who have been humiliated, brought low, the victims of violence and those who find themselves on the margins of society: "In arrogance the wicked persecute the poor—/ let them be caught in the schemes they have devised" (10:2); "'Because the poor are despoiled, because the needy groan,/ I will now rise up,' says the LORD" (12:5). If poverty is not held up as an ascetic ideal, it is because it is accompanied, in real life, by a feeling of helplessness, misery, and unhappiness. The psalms evoke the various avatars of poverty that add to the suffering of humankind: "As for me, I am poor and needy" (40:17; see also 70:5; 86:1; 109:22); "Consider my affliction [poverty] and my trouble" (25:18); "Wretched [poor] and close to death from my youth up" (88:15).

Fortunately, the poor know how to touch the heart of God and receive God's comfort and support in any circumstances: "You would confound the plans of the poor,/ but the LORD is their refuge" (14:6); "This poor soul cried, and was heard by the LORD,/ and was saved from every trouble" (34:6); "For he delivers the needy when they call,/ the poor and those who have no helper./ He has pity on the weak and the needy,/ and saves the lives of the needy./ From oppression and violence he redeems their life;/ and precious is their blood in his sight" (72:12-14).

The psalms not only speak of some ultimate recourse for the poor in the life to come, they urgently plead for justice and advocacy on behalf of the poor in the here and now. The king, too, is expected to do his part: "May he [the king] judge your people with righteousness,/ and your poor with justice" (72:2). The powerful of this world are called upon too: "Give justice to the weak and the orphan;/ maintain the right of the lowly and the destitute" (82:3). And the same is expected of all of us who believe: "Happy are those who consider the poor;/ the LORD delivers them in the day of trouble" (41:1).

Although it is emphatically rejected, the experience of poverty remains, nevertheless, and paradox, a crucible in which the human heart learns to seek God. The poor know how to hope and to open their hearts to the salvation that comes from God: "The helpless commit themselves to you;/ you have been the helper of the orphan./ O LORD, you will hear the desire of the meek;/ you will strengthen their heart" (10:14, 17); "Let the oppressed see it and be glad;/ you who seek God, let your hearts revive" (69:32). Because they seek God, they will not be disappointed and they will receive the earth as their inheritance: "But the meek shall inherit the land,/ and delight themselves in abundant prosperity" (37:11).

PRAISE

HALLEL   הלל

Hallel	
Total OT	206
1. Ps	119
2. Isa	16
3. 2 Chr	13

1. Root

Out of the 119 occurrences of this root in its various combinations in the psalms, the verb *hallal* occurs 89 times, and the derived noun *tehillah* (praise) 30 times. These numbers make the Psalter the book of the praise of God par excellence. Cognate roots in other ancient Semitic languages mean to cry out for joy, to acclaim. In the Bible, the verb *hallal* is sometimes used in response to some particularly noble human traits (Gen 12:15; 2 Sam 14:25; Prov 12:8), but it is a word that is generally directed toward God.

2. Usage

The root occurs throughout the psalms, but most often in the last third of the book (Psalms 100–150). Here we find the form alleluia ("Praise the Lord!") used twenty-three times. These last fifty psalms contain a whole battery of songs of praise, ending in the final crescendo of the last three (Psalms 148–150) with 28 occurrences of the root.

It is praise that really defines the climate of prayer of the Psalter. Whereas other types of prayer are more circumstantial, praise is always in season: "I will bless the LORD at all times;/ his praise shall continually be in my mouth" (34:1); "Every day I will bless you,/ and praise your name forever and ever" (145:2).

This is so because praise by its essence belongs to and is directed toward God, who merits praise just for being God: "Praise is due to you, O God, in Zion" (65:1); "Great is the LORD, and greatly to be praised;/ his greatness is unsearchable" (145:3); "Praise the LORD!/ O give thanks to the LORD, for he is good;/ for his steadfast love endures forever./ Who can utter the mighty doings of the LORD,/ or declare all his praise?" (106:1-2).

The praise of the psalmists flowed from a profound experience of God; it was nourished as well by the countless marvels of creation. While blessings and acts of thanksgiving are generally directed toward God for particular marvelous events and "great deeds" in the history of Israel's salvation, praise is principally—but not exclusively—the response to the beauty, the grandeur, and the goodness of creation: "Praise the LORD!/ Praise the LORD from the heavens;/ praise him in the heights!/ Praise him, sun and moon;/ praise him, all you shining stars!/ Praise the LORD from the earth" (148:1, 3, 7).

To be moved to praise God one does not need to have experienced some extraordinary rescue in a dire crisis; one only to open the eyes and see the immensity of creation, made from nothing: "Let heaven and earth praise him,/ the seas and everything that moves in them" (69:34). Above all, we praise God for the gift of life and make of our entire existence an act of praise: "Let everything that breathes praise the LORD!" (150:6).

Finally, it is communal praise that is the purest expression of this form of prayer, as we see from the predominance of the plural form of the verb (some 50x. out of 89). Even when the words of praise are spoken by an individual, the community is invoked: "I will tell of your name to my brothers and sisters;/ in the midst of the congregation I will praise you" (22:22).

PRAYER

TEFILLAH תפלה

Tefillah	
Total OT	77
1. Ps	32
2. 2 Chr	12
3. 1 Kgs	8
Other Forms	79

1. Root

Hebrew vocabulary for everything to do with prayer is particularly rich and flexible, and this is seen especially well in the Psalter. However, the word *tefillah* appears as a key word that could almost be called technical. The other words seem to gravitate around this one. The original meaning of the root from which it is derived, *palal,* is disputed. In the last century it was held to be cognate with Arabic *falla,* which means to cut oneself, to wound oneself. The connection would be that cutting oneself was thought to be a means of inducing a state of ecstasy. A second hypothesis makes the word a close cousin of a similar-sounding verb, *nafal* (to fall). In this case, it means that one prostrates oneself to pray. In the Bible, the verb *palal* is most often found in the reflexive conjugation, with the meaning of praying for, interceding (Gen 20:7, 17; Deut 9:20, 26).

2. *Usage*

Tefillah is found five times in the Psalter as the introductory title of an individual psalm: prayer of David (17:1; 86:1; 142:1), of Moses (90:1), of one afflicted when faint and pleading before the Lord (102:1). It is found once as a summing up of a collection of psalms: prayers of David (72:20).

Prayer covers a vast array of experiences, if we can judge from the terms that are used to parallel *tefillah*. Prayer can be a cry (4:2; 5:3; 88:14; 102:2), a complaint (17:1; 61:2; 88:3), a supplication (6:10; 55:2; 86:6; 143:1); it can be actual words (54:4), or a song (42:9), or even an instruction (142:1).

Because it is so adaptable, prayer arises naturally at all the most significant turns of life. Felt as a real need in times of distress (32:6), prayer is also the mainstay of everyday life, a vital practice for the believer. It arises in the psalmist's heart during the whole day, from the morning to the evening: "But I, O LORD, cry out to you;/ in the morning my prayer comes before you" (88:13; see also 5:3-4); "Let my prayer be counted as incense before you,/ and the lifting up of my hands as an evening sacrifice" (141:2). Prayer is not limited to the day; it arises in the night, in response to a day filled with the love of God: "By day the LORD commands his steadfast love,/ and at night his song is with me,/ a prayer to the God of my life" (42:8).

In the Psalter we find the practice of prayer, rather than its theory. There is little in the way of advice, principles, or techniques. The one criterion for prayer seems to be truth: "Give ear to my prayer from lips free from deceit" (17:1). Aside from that one condition, nothing is censured or restricted: prayer arises spontaneously in situations of distress, anguish, injustice, unhappiness, and just as freely in times of happiness and celebration.

Although the prayer of the psalms is permeated with praise, it nonetheless has a very important dramatic character. Prayer often arises in extremely difficult and even tormented conditions: "O LORD God of hosts,/ how long will you be angry with your people's prayers?" (80:4); "O LORD, why do you cast me off?/ Why do you hide your face from me?" (88:14).

PSALM

MIZMOR מזמור

Mizmor	
Total OT	57
Ps	57
Other Forms	55

1. Root

This word, found only in the Psalter, derives from the root *zamar*. The verb *zimmer*, typical of the language of the psalms (41 occurrences out of 45 in the Old Testament), means to make music, to play an instrument, or to sing. So as a religious poem and a prayer, a psalm is first of all sung or accompanied by an instrument.

2. Usage

The word always appears in the title at the beginning of a psalm (Psalm 3–6; 8–9; 12–13; etc.). *Shir* (song) appears next in frequency, at the beginning of thirty psalms (45; 46; 120–134). Both words are often found near each other in the same verse (30:1; 48:1; 65:1; 66:1; 67:1; 68:1). So more than half of the psalms (87 out of 150) have titles that have something to do with music and singing. If we add to this the numerous musical annotations in the titles (musical instruments and melodies), as well as all the references to music within the psalm itself, we must conclude that the Psalter developed, at least originally, in a musical context.

The psalms of Israel were intended to be sung. How, for instance, could one recite Psalm 47 without entering into the joyous and enthusiastic rhythm that enlivens it: "Clap your hands, all you peoples;/ shout to God with loud songs of joy./ God has gone up with a shout,/ the LORD with the sound of a trumpet./ Sing praises to God, sing praises;/ sing praises to our King, sing praises./ For God is the king of all the earth;/ sing praises with a psalm" (47:1, 5-7)? Without music and lively ovations this psalm would never have been composed.

This is, then, one of the major problems faced with the use of the psalms today: the musical dimension is often ignored or, at best, downplayed. We often just say the words without even hearing the music, and this rarely does the words justice. We say the word "Sing!" and we do everything but. We say "Dance!" and of course do nothing of the kind; it would be unthinkable in our assemblies or prayer groups. We say "Play the harp" and there are no instruments in our churches. This happens when we say or recite the psalms, which were intended to be sung.

We should, on the contrary, bring in all our musical resources (instruments, songs, refrains, choirs, acclamations, dances, etc.) and then, and only then, will we truly be experiencing the spirit that gave birth to the psalms in all their joyousness and festivity, as well as their sadness and plaintiveness. "O sing to the LORD a new song. . . ./ Make a joyful noise to the LORD, all the earth;/ break forth into joyous song and sing praises./ Sing praises to the LORD with the lyre,/ with the lyre and the sound of melody./ With trumpets and the sound of the horn/ make a joyful noise before the King, the LORD" (98:1, 4-6).

REJOICE

SAMACH   שׂמח

Samach	
Total OT	269
1. Ps	68
2. Prov	28
3. Isa	25

1. Root

The religion of Israel, with its festivals, music, and dancing, places great emphasis on joy and celebration. So it is no surprise that the vocabulary of joy is very well represented in the Psalter. We find the verb *samach* (rejoice) in the psalms fifty-two times, the adjective *sameach* (joyful) three times, and the noun *simchah* (joy) thirteen times. The Psalter also has a good number of synonyms: *sis* (rejoice) and its derivatives (12 occurrences out of an Old Testament total of 65, in second place after Isaiah, which has 24 occurrences), *gil* (exult; 22 uses out of a total of 55, with the greatest frequency of the Old

Testament), and *ranan* (jubilate; in first position again, with 42 occurrences out of a total of 91).

2. *Usage*

The psalms bring out what could be called the paschal character of joy—the passing over from tears to laughter, from suffering to healing, from sterility to fertility, from death to life, all made possible by God.

However, we find only one allusion to the kind of joy afforded by ordinary life that the Sages teach us to appreciate (see especially Proverbs and Ecclesiastes): it is the joy that comes from "wine to gladden the human heart" (104:15). In all the other occurrences the joy of the psalmists does not represent an attitude of vague and naive optimism, but it is the fruit of a long and arduous war waged against suffering and death: "You have turned my mourning into dancing;/ you have taken off my sackcloth/ and clothed me with joy" (30:11; see also 31:8; 51:10). Such joy arises from a radical change in circumstances, where God intervenes in human affairs to change, for instance, the humiliation of sterility into the joy of maternity. The woman who was sterile becomes "the joyous mother of children" (113:9).

Of all these sudden divine reversals of fortune, the return from exile was certainly the one that gave rise to the most vibrant manifestations of joy, one that had been long awaited: "When the LORD restores the fortunes of his people,/ Jacob will rejoice; Israel will be glad" (14:7). And when the dream became reality, there was an explosion of joy: "When the LORD restored the fortunes of Zion,/ we were like those who dream./ Then our mouth was filled with laughter,/ and our tongue with shouts of joy" (126:1-2). The paschal dimension of joy that is so characteristic of the psalms is clearly expressed in a well-known adage: "May those who sow in tears/ reap with shouts of joy *[rinnah]*./ Those who go out weeping,/ bearing the seed for sowing,/ shall come home with shouts of joy,/ carrying their sheaves" (126:5-6).

As important as joy is in daily life, it is especially appropriate in worship: "Then I will go to the altar of God,/ to God my exceeding joy" (43:4); "Worship the LORD with gladness;/ come into his presence with singing" (100:2).

The joy of God is mentioned only once in the Psalter, in a psalm of creation, expressing admirably the pleasure that the Lord took upon gazing at the work of his hands (Genesis 1): "May the glory of the LORD endure forever;/ may the LORD rejoice in his works" (104:31).

SAVE

YASHA^c ישע

Yasha^c	
Total OT	354
1. Ps	136
2. Isa	56
3. Judg	22

1. Root

Yasha^c is undoubtedly one of the most familiar of Hebrew roots to Christians, thanks to a number of proper names that are derived from it: Joshua *(Yehoshu^ca)*, Hosea *(Hoshe^ca)*, Isaiah *(Yesha^cyahu)*, Josiah, and Jesus *(Yeshu^ca)*, and also the liturgical acclamation *"hosanna!"* ("give salvation!"; Matt 21:9; see also Ps 118:25).

The verb *yasha^c* means to be spacious, wide, vast, and is used as the opposite of the concept of oppression and narrowness (anguish, in its original sense, from the Latin *angustia*, narrow place, defile). Most often found in the causative conjugation, it came to mean to set free, to make room, to free, to liberate. Liberation and salvation are seen as giving a person room, after having been squeezed into a tight place (see Ps 18:20; 118:5). The root gave rise to three nouns as well that are found in the Psalter: *yesha^c* (20x.), *yeshu^cah* (45x.), and *teshu^cah* (13x.), all meaning salvation.

Generally speaking, the word salvation does not have in the Old Testament the spiritual connotation that it assumes in the New Testament and in Christian theology: forgiveness of sins, liberation from the hold of evil and from Satan. It means rather deliverance from a specific danger, from a catastrophe, or from a concrete, visible enemy. It is often encountered in a military context (which explains its 22 occurrences in Judges), where it actually means victory.

2. Usage

This concrete meaning of salvation emerges from a number of psalms. God delivers from the aggressor, the enemy, or from bodily dangers and anguish: "O LORD my God, in you I take refuge;/ save me from all my pursuers, and deliver me" (7:1); "Wondrously show your steadfast love,/ O savior of those who seek refuge" (17:7); "I call upon the LORD, who is worthy to be praised,/ so I shall be saved from my enemies" (18:3); "Save me from the mouth of the lion!/ From the horns of the wild oxen you have rescued me" (22:21); "Save me, O God,/ for the waters have come up to my neck" (69:1); "Though I walk in the midst of trouble,/ you preserve me against the wrath of my enemies;/ . . . and your right hand delivers me" (138:7).

In a good number of places salvation means the victorious outcome of a battle or other confrontation (76:10; 108:7) and can be translated simply as victory: "May we shout for joy over your victory. . . ./ Now I know that the LORD will help his anointed;/ he will answer him from his holy heaven/ with mighty victories by his right hand. . . ./ Give victory to the king, O LORD" (20:5-6, 9). Attributing military victory to the support of God, while well-intended, can lead to ambiguity, however, and there is some danger in appropriating God's approval to one's every cause. Surely such an attitude gets in the way of a higher will that all peoples live together in harmony and justice.

When they returned from exile, salvation for the people of Israel took the form of reconstruction and the regathering of the tribes: "For God will save Zion/ and rebuild the cities of Judah" (69:35); "Save us, O LORD our God,/ and gather us from among the nations" (106:47). Around the same time Psalm 51, reflecting the influence of Jeremiah and the Deuteronomist school, begins to express a more interiorized concept of salvation relating to the forgiveness of sins: "Wash me thoroughly from my iniquity. . . ./ Restore to me the joy of your salvation" (51:2, 12).

SEEK

BIQQESH בקש

Biqqesh	
Total OT	225
1. Ps	27
2. 1 Sam	26
3. Jer	23
Other Forms	8

1. Root

Biqqesh is a well-known Semitic root with a well-established meaning: seeking either persons or objects, concrete or abstract. It is only used in the Bible in the intensive conjugation, which effectively emphasizes the intensity of the person's involvement in seeking something.

2. Usage

Seeking is understood, first of all, as a daily and sustained activity. An example would be the seeking of food: "I have not seen the righteous forsaken/ or their children begging [seeking] bread" (37:25). Another example is the choice of two opposing options, deceit or peace: "How long, you people, shall my honor suffer shame?/ How long will you love vain words, and seek after lies?" (4:2); "Depart from evil and do good;/ seek peace, and pursue it" (34:14).

The just must always face the wiles of the adversary and the plots of all those who seek his or her harm (71:13, 24) to the point of plotting murder (35:4; 37:32; 38:12; etc.).

Of course, the most profound seeking takes place on a religious level: one seeks the face of God (24:6; 27:8; 105:4). The participle is used to designate a well-defined group, those who seek God: "But may all who seek you/ rejoice and be glad in you" (40:16); "Do not let those who seek you be dishonored because of me,/ O God of Israel" (69:6); "Let the hearts of those who seek the LORD rejoice" (105:3). The expression is known in other Semitic languages, where it refers to the activity of the pilgrims who come to see the face of their gods, represented by statues. These statues were forbidden in the religion of Israel, so this expression lost its concrete meaning in Hebrew. But seeking God always occupied a privileged place in the Temple-centered religion: "One thing I asked of the

LORD,/ that will I seek after:/ to live in the house of the LORD/ all the days of my life" (27:4).

By definition, the act of seeking is an ongoing and unfinished activity. It is an act that is lived through a continual process of self-questioning and of discoveries that demand inner renewal: "'Come,' my heart says, 'Seek his face!'/ Your face, LORD, do I seek./ Do not hide your face from me" (27:8-9); "Seek the LORD and his strength;/ seek his presence continually" (105:4).

Only in one instance is God the subject of the verb to seek, but there it has a meaning that is a delightful foretaste of the parable of the good shepherd: "I have gone astray like a lost sheep; seek out your servant" (119:176).

SHEOL
(THE ABODE OF THE DEAD)

SHEᵓOL   שָׁאוֹל

Sheᵓol	
Total OT	66
1. Ps	16
2. Isa	10
3. Prov	9

1. Root

The origin of this word remains obscure. It might derive from the well-known biblical root shaᵓal (to demand, to require); the abode of the dead would then demand or require the life of every human being. Another explanation derives it from the root shaᵓal (to be deep; this root occurs 4x. in the Old Testament), with the resultant meaning of pit or abyss, so that the abode of the dead would be an underground place. The notion of an abode of the dead is close to the concept of the Assyrians and the Babylonians, and, to a somewhat lesser degree, to the Greek Hades.

2. Usage

The Sheol of the Israelites does not have the negative connotation of hell. It is part of their idea of the universe (sky, earth, sea, etc.), and, as such, does not escape the universal presence of God: "If I ascend to heaven, you are there;/ if I make my bed in Sheol, you are there" (139:8).

Originally, *she'ol* means the sojourn of the dead, all the dead, the just and unjust alike, without distinction: "Who can live and never see death?/ Who can escape the power of Sheol?" (89:48). There is no corresponding positive place for the just who have died; *she'ol* is the one and only kingdom of death, the ultimate and universal resting place from which no one can escape (6:6; 18:6; 49:15; 55:16; 89:49; 116:3). Little is known of this place, except that it leads to a somehow diminished and shadowy existence, in dust and silence, with no relationship with God (88:6, 11-13).

But the term gradually came to mean the lot of the impious and the evil: "The wicked shall depart to Sheol" (9:17); "Let the wicked be put to shame;/ let them go dumbfounded to Sheol" (31:17); "Like sheep they are appointed for Sheol;/ Death shall be their shepherd;/ straight to the grave they descend,/ and their form shall waste away;/ Sheol shall be their home" (49:14; see also 55:16).

From this conception of the lot of the wicked we see arise all those prayers of the just to be spared such a fate, and the hope of being delivered from the bonds of death: "The snares of death encompassed me;/ the pangs of Sheol laid hold on me;/ I suffered distress and anguish./ Then I called on the name of the LORD:/ 'O LORD, I pray, save my life!'" (116:3-4; see also 18:5-7; 88:3-4).

While we cannot pretend to find any certitude or elaborated doctrine on the subject of the afterlife in the Old Testament and the Psalter, we do find examples of courage and serenity in total surrender to God: "For you do not give me up to Sheol,/ or let your faithful one see the Pit" (16:10); "O LORD, you brought up my soul from Sheol,/ restored me to life from among those gone down to the Pit" (30:3); "For great is your steadfast love toward me;/ you have delivered my soul from the depths of Sheol" (86:13; see also 49:16; 73:23-24). It was from such glimmerings of hope that the Jews first developed their faith in the resurrection of the dead (translation of the psalms into Greek, toward 250 B.C.E., the birth of the Pharisaic movement, the Jewish apocrypha), and the early Christians eventually followed (see the missionary speeches of the Acts of the Apostles).

SIN

CHATA' חטא

Chata'	
Total OT	593
1. Lev	116
2. Num	67
3. 1 Kgs	42
6. Ps	34

1. Root

The original meaning of *chata'* is to miss the mark, as is seen, for instance, when speaking of warriors in Judges 20:16: "Every one could sling a stone at a hair, and not miss [literally, and not sin]." It implies the idea of falling to one side, of missing the goal (see also Ps 25:8, 51:15; those who have fallen by the wayside— "sinners in the way"). Although there are about fifty or so related words for the idea of sin, it is the root *chata'* around which the biblical notion of sin crystallized.

2. Usage

The root is used thirty-four times in the Psalms, with the psalmists confessing to sin, fearing it, or denouncing it. But there is not a clear idea of what sin is. We can, nevertheless, point to two dimensions of the sinful act. The first belongs to the realm of human relations: "Do not sweep me away with sinners,/ nor my life with the bloodthirsty,/ those in whose hands are evil devices,/ and whose right hands are full of bribes" (26:9-10). The second involves our relations (or non-relations) with God: "Yet they sinned still more against him,/ rebelling against the Most High in the desert" (78:17); "In spite of all this they still sinned;/ they did not believe in his wonders" (78:32). What is essential to the nature of sin is clear: we sin against humankind when we commit violence and injustice; we sin against God when we refuse the divine gift of freedom of action.

The psalmists exhibit an acute yet wholesome sense of the unavoidable and sad experience of sin: "Then I acknowledged my sin to you,/ and I did not hide my iniquity" (32:5); "There is no soundness in my flesh/ because of your indignation;/ there is no health in my bones/ because of my sin" (38:3); "I confess my iniquity;/ I am sorry for my sin" (38:18); "For I know my transgressions,/ and my sin is ever before me" (51:3).

What we have here is an acute sense of sinfulness, but not one that leads to helplessness and despair. On the contrary, out of the full consciousness of the misery brought on by their sin, the psalmists cry out all the more boldly to God, asking for the free gift of pardon: "Do not remember the sins of my youth or my transgressions" (25:7); "Consider my affliction and my trouble,/ and forgive all my sins" (25:18); "As for me, I said, 'O LORD, be gracious to me;/ heal me, for I have sinned against you'" (41:4); "Wash me thoroughly from my iniquity,/ and cleanse me from my sin" (51:2); "Hide your face from my sins" (51:9); "Deliver us, and forgive our sins,/ for your name's sake" (79:9).

God's forgiveness is not only something hoped for and long awaited. Both individuals and the whole people have firsthand experience of God's pardon and can bear witness to the Good News of God's forgiveness: "Happy are those whose transgression is forgiven,/ whose sin is covered" (32:1); "You forgave the iniquity of your people;/ you pardoned all their sin" (85:2); "He does not deal with us according to our sins,/ nor repay us according to our iniquities" (103:10; see also vv. 11-12). And even though it remains difficult for humans to forgive one another, the experience of God's renewed forgiveness leads the psalmist to go through life with more understanding of the ways of the Lord, and enables him to teach these ways to his fellow-sinners: "Then I will teach transgressors your ways,/ and sinners will return to you" (51:13).

SOUL

NEFESH נפש

Nefesh	
Total OT	754
1. Ps	144
2. Jer	62
3. Lev	60
Other Forms	3

1. Root

Here we have one of the major concepts of biblical anthropology: *nefesh,* which is usually translated as soul. The Greek translation of the Septuagint interpreted it in this sense in almost six hundred instances (translating it as *psyche*). In doing so, the Septuagint reflects the influence of Greek philosophy that gave the Christian world the basic concepts with which it elaborated its doctrine of the supernatural world.

The temptation to interpret this word as soul in this philosophical sense is therefore great. This would lead us to understand the soul as a reality distinct from the body, or even as opposed to what is corporeal: the soul is immortal, subtle, and invisible, while the body is mortal, concrete, and visible. But this way of thinking is totally foreign to the psalmists and the biblical authors. They shared a unitary vision of the human being, as opposed to a dichotomized or dualistic view. A human being is body and soul in one.

2. Usage

The *nefesh* is the very opposite of an immaterial and subtle substance. *Nefesh,* in fact, concretely designates a physical part of the human being—the throat (or the gullet) or the neck: "For he satisfies the thirsty [literally, he satisfies their gullet],/ and the hungry he fills with good things [literally, he fills the gullet of the hungry]" (107:9). The *nefesh* is therefore the particular location of sensations such as hunger, thirst, and taste. It follows logically that it is also the central organ of hunger and longing. So the *nefesh* stands for the human being in a situation of want and necessity. When we speak of "soul," we mean the human being as a desiring being. It is an easy step to make the *nefesh* the symbol of the thirst for God: "As a deer longs for flowing streams,/ so my soul longs for you, O God" (42:1).

The *nefesh* is the whole life of the psalmist: "For my soul is full of troubles,/ and my life draws near to Sheol" (88:3). This meaning often appears in a context of mortal danger. God keeps or saves the *nefesh* from death, that is, God saves the life of the faithful: "O LORD, you brought up my soul from Sheol,/ restored me to life from among those gone down to the Pit" (30:3; see also 16:10). When the psalmist speaks of lifting his soul to God, it is in fact his entire existence that he means to place before God: "Gladden the soul of your servant,/ for to you, O Lord, I lift up my soul" (86:4).

We also find the more specific sense of the word for soul as the seat and location of psychological impressions. For the psalmist the soul is, in fact, the site of emotions such as anxiety, grief, and joy: "My soul also is struck with terror" (6:3); "Then my soul shall rejoice in the LORD" (35:9); "My soul is cast down within me" (42:6) and "Why are you cast down, O my soul,/ and why are you disquieted within me?" (42:11).

But even here the soul is not part of the human being, but the whole of the human from the aspect of desire. For this reason the translators often use a personal pronoun instead of the word soul: "They repay me [my soul] evil for good" (35:12).

THANKSGIVING

YADAH   ידה

Yadah	
Total OT	111
1. Ps	67
2. 1 Chr	9
3. 2 Chr	8
Other Forms	33

1. Root

The name Judah *(Yehuda)* comes from this root, according to the passage in Genesis where his mother Leah gives birth to him and cries out: "'This time I will praise the LORD'; therefore she named him Judah" (Gen 29:35). Besides the verb forms, the Old Testament uses the noun *todah* thirty-two times in all

(12 in the Psalter), a noun that refers to a particular practice of prayer and thanksgiving sacrifice (50:14, 23; 107:22; 116:17). The meaning of the verb *yadah* is very close to that of the verb *hallal* (to praise) and its derivatives, and the two verbs are often found in a parallel construction (35:18; 44:9; 100:4; 106:47; 109:30; etc.). Most translations use "give thanks," so that the meaning of thanking and gratitude is conveyed. But the verb *yadah* can also be found in the penitential psalms with the meaning of confessing one's faults, and can take on the broader meaning of public avowal, proclamation (32:5).

2. Usage

A look at the structure of the psalms of thanksgiving (18, 30, 31, 40, 66, 67, 92, 107, 116, 118) will afford us a better understanding of the meaning and significance of the verb *yadah*. Let us consider first Psalm 118. The psalm opens and ends with an invitation to the community to listen to the witness of a believer and to join with him in "confessing" God and the wonders the Lord has accomplished for him: "O give thanks to the LORD, for he is good,/ his steadfast love endures forever!" (118:29). The body of the psalm is the story of the distress in which he had been plunged and the intervention of God who saved him (118:5-18). The psalm continues with a dialogue between the faithful person and the community, ending with the festive acclamation of the divine name (188:19-28).

So giving thanks is much more than a private act of an individual, expressing his or her gratitude to God. It is an act that expresses one's faith and the faith of the community: "Then I will thank you in the great congregation;/ in the mighty throng I will praise you" (35:18); "With my mouth I will give great thanks to the LORD;/ I will praise him in the midst of the throng" (109:30). This public "confession," which always includes the story of the faithful's salvation, may end with a song: "I will give to the LORD the thanks due to his righteousness,/ and sing praise to the name of the LORD, the Most High" (7:17; see also 18:50; 30:5; 33:2; 92:2). To confess God is first of all to proclaim the divine name. But it also means that the faithful who has had concrete experience of God's saving act can draw lessons that are valid for the entire community of believers: "It is better to take refuge in the LORD than to put confidence in mortals./ It is better to take refuge in the LORD than to put confidence in princes./ The stone that the builders rejected/ has become the chief cornerstone" (118:8-9, 22).

The act of thanksgiving is distinguished from that of praise in that it arises from a specific event, a particular intervention of God on behalf of the psalmist: "You have turned my mourning into dancing;/ you have taken off my sackcloth/ and clothed me with joy,/ so that my soul may praise you and not be silent./ O LORD my God, I will give thanks to you forever" (30:11-12; see also 138:1-3).

TRUST

BATACH בטח

Batach	
Total OT	182
1. Ps	52
2. Isa	26
3. Jer	23

1. Root

The Septuagint translates the verb *batach* as *elpizein* (to hope) rather than as *pistuein* (to believe). But the Hebrew word indicates more the interior, subjective disposition of trustingness felt toward a person, rather than the objective response of one's intelligence or will to the contents of a revelation. If we were to think of it as having faith, it would have to be a trusting faith. Somewhat surprisingly, this word has a negative sense when applied to relationships between humans, where it often connotes over-trustingness, to the point of credulity and gullibility; whereas it has a totally positive sense when applied to trust in God.

2. Usage

As elsewhere in the Bible, trust, for the psalmists, is directed most often toward God. There are only ten references to trust in any other relationship, and in each of these instances trust is denounced as being deceptive. We are to put all our trust in God alone. Even our friends can go over to the other camp: "Even my bosom friend in whom I trusted,/ who ate of my bread, has lifted the heel against me" (41:9). At the perspective of the ultimate ruin of the "strong man," the just will recognize some day the fact that great riches do not avail: "See the one who would not take refuge in God,/ but trusted in abundant riches, and sought refuge in wealth!" (52:7; see also 49:7). The same is true of those who put their trust in weapons (44:7) and trickery (62:11), which all ultimately fail. There is one inescapable conclusion: "It is better to take refuge in the LORD/ than to put confidence in mortals./ It is better to take refuge in the LORD/ than to put confidence in princes" (118:8-9; see also 146:3).

The noun *betach* appears three times with the meaning of security: "I will both lie down and sleep in peace;/ for you alone, O LORD, make me lie down in safety" (4:8); "Therefore my heart is glad, and my soul rejoices;/ my body also rests secure" (16:9); "He led them in safety, so that they were not afraid" (78:53). It has been said, with justification, that, for the authors of the Bible, faith *was* hope, in the sense that faith is placed in persons, and not in any abstractions like truths or dogmas. This assertion is supported by the use of the noun *mibtach*, which is translated in the liturgy as both faith and hope: "Happy are those who make the LORD their trust" (40:4); "By awesome deeds you answer us with deliverance,/ O God of our salvation;/ you are the hope of all the ends of the earth" (65:5). The third and last use of the word in the Psalter confirms the meaning of hope, while *mibtach* is paralleled with *tiqwah*, which means hope precisely: "For you, O Lord, are my hope,/ my trust, O LORD, from my youth" (71:5).

Trust is interpersonal: one relies on God or turns toward God. But there are helps along the way to such utter trust: it can repose on the certitude of God's love for us (13:6; 52:10), God's holy name (33:21), God's saving power (78:22), or God's word (119:42).

TRUTH

ʾEMET אמת

ʾEmet	
Total OT	330
1. Ps	84
2. Isa	34
3. Deut	23

1. Root

Although it remains difficult to establish the original meaning of the root ʾaman in the ancient Semitic languages that are even older than Hebrew, when we compare it with cognates in Arabic and Syriac, the basic meaning of the root is to be solid, to be firm, to last. It is found in the Old Testament in the simple verb form applied to people—women and men—to whom particular responsibilities are entrusted (Num 11:12; 2 Kgs 10:1, 5). In the passive or reflexive forms, the verb, when applied to things, takes on the meaning of hard, lasting, firm (Isa 33:16; Jer 15:18); when applied to people, it means trustworthy, reliable (Prov 25:13; Isa 8:2; 49:7; Deut 7:9). In the causative conjugation the verb means to believe. In its profane sense it is used in a negative context: to doubt, to distrust (Prov 14:15; 26:25). It is also used for the incredulity that the people often succumb to (Exod 4:30-31; 14:31; 19:9).

We find as well two nouns derived from the verb: ʾemet (usually translated as truth) and ʾemunah, which the Septuagint translates as *pistis* (faith). In both cases the word translates a highly regarded human quality (Prov 3:3; 12:19; 22:21) or a value found in its perfect form only in God (2 Sam 7:28; Isa 61:8; Jer 32:41). What is most remarkable is that the word in the Bible never refers to some abstraction, to truth as an idea, but always to the concrete solidity of things, to the trustworthiness of a word once given, and to the reliability of persons.

The well-known response ʾamen occurs twenty-four times in the Old Testament to express the people's or an individual's adherence to the Word of God (a promise, a curse, or a mission): Deuteronomy 27:15-26; Numbers 5:21-22; Jeremiah 11:5. And the word already has a liturgical character as the people's response to a prayer (Neh 8:6; 1 Chr 16:36).

2. Usage

The psalms sing first and foremost of the *'emet* of God: "O send out your light and your truth;/ let them lead me" (43:3); "I will also praise you with the harp/ for your faithfulness, O my God" (71:22); "Righteousness and justice are the foundation of your throne;/ steadfast love and faithfulness go before you" (89:14). To speak of the truth of the faithfulness of God is to say that one has utter confidence in God, that one knows God's word is solid and believable.

Recalling the flight from Egypt and the wanderings of Israel in the desert, the psalms remind us again and again of the vacillations of the people, torn between faith and doubt, between fidelity and disobedience. For a long time they resisted the gift of freedom that was offered to them, and often they fell prey to fear: "Because they had no faith in God,/ and did not trust his saving power" (78:22); "In spite of all this they still sinned;/ they did not believe in his wonders" (78:32).

Further, it is clear that faith implies concrete actions (one walks in faith or is led in faith) and that faith is a gift freely given. Those who believe address God, asking God to teach them to believe and to guide them in the faith: "Make me to know your ways, O LORD;/ teach me your paths" (25:4); "For your steadfast love is before my eyes,/ and I walk in faithfulness to you" (26:3).

WAY (PATH)

DEREK דרך

Derek	
Total OT	706
1. Ezek	107
2. Prov	75
3. Ps	66
Other Forms	62

1. Root

In the narrative parts of the Bible (from Genesis to 2 Kings), the word *derek* is usually used in its spatial sense: the road, the path that one treads, as well as traveling and voyages (Gen 3:24; 30:36; 31:23; 38:14; etc.). But it is also used figuratively, as the direction one takes in life, either according to the will of God or against it (Deut 5:33; 9:12, 16; 11:28; 30:16; 31:29). The word also acquires an important symbolic meaning in the great epic of Exodus, where it stands for the wanderings of Israel, the long and hard march to safety and freedom from Egypt to the land of Canaan (Exod 3:18; 13:21; Deut 1:31; Josh 24:17: "He [God] protected us along all the way that we went, and among all the peoples through whom we passed."

2. Usage

For the psalmists, the world is separated into two parts. There are not an infinite number of choices, only two: "The LORD watches over the way of the righteous,/ but the way of the wicked will perish" (1:6). There is no middle ground, there are no shades of meaning. One of these two paths must be chosen.

The wisdom psalms and the individual lamentations refer to both the quiet search for the right way and the painful gropings of the one who is still seeking the way. For "way," we must also understand the destiny of the seeker after enlightenment ("Teach me your way, O LORD,/ and lead me on a level path," 27:11; see also 86:11; 119:33), as well as the destiny we have chosen for ourselves through our life choices, for good or for ill: "They [the wicked] are set on a way that is not good" (36:4); "Commit your way to the LORD" (37:5).

In several places the psalms speak of a collective path, sometimes marked by faith and sometimes by error, but always led on by invitations to walk with God: "O that my people would listen to me,/ that Israel would walk in my ways!" (81:13; see also 44:18; 95:10).

Finally, there are God's ways of acting and of leading history: "This God—his way is perfect" (18:30); "Your way, O God, is holy" (77:13); "They shall sing of the ways of the LORD,/ for great is the glory of the LORD" (138:5); "The LORD is just in all his ways" (145:17). In these texts the way of the Lord refers to the Lord's habitual way of acting. Still, these ways remain mysterious. Even when they are revealed ("He has made known his ways to Moses," 103:7), they are often misunderstood or not understood at all: "They are a people whose hearts go astray,/ and they do not regard my ways" (95:10).

If we add to the word *derek* the meanings path, walking, climbing (see the psalms of ascent, 120–134), we are obliged to concur that the psalms present us with a spirituality of pilgrimage and journey. We cannot stop and rest on our laurels. We must keep journeying toward the Promised Land, remembering that God is always ahead: "O God, when you went out before your people,/ when you marched through the wilderness,/ the earth quaked" (68:7-8).

WICKED

RASHA^c רשע

Rasha^c	
Total OT	343
1. Ps	92
2. Prov	87
3. Job	40

1. Root

The root *rasha^c* means, in the active, to act falsely or to declare guilt. It occurs most often in the Bible in the adjective form *rasha^c* (wicked or impious), often found in opposition to the adjective *tsaddiq* (just). In the rest of the Bible outside of the Psalter, it is found mainly in the sapiential works, where the wickedness of sinners is described in absolutist terms to contrast justice and evil.

2. Usage

The whole drama of the psalms is played out in the opposition between the just person and the wicked. A. Chouraqui has described the dramatic scene vividly: "The two actors in this duel between life and death, facing each other from start to finish, are the Innocent and the Rebel. They each refuse to give in. One rejects the way of light; the other, the way of darkness. One says no to the iniquity of the world; the other refuses the eternity of God. These refusals are at the heart of the tragedy. This conflict between two opposing wills, possible because of their essential freedom, is the source of the horror which erupts into the world and wounds the joy of creation."[1]

Who are these wicked? For C. Van Leeuwen there are three possibilities: (1) the enemy peoples in the Bible (the enemies of the king or of Israel); (2) the powerful who oppress the poor and the weak; (3) former friends who betray.[2]

We get a clearer idea of the nature of the wicked in the psalms from the words used in apposition or in parallel construction. In general, they are described as sinners (1:1; 104:35) and the workers of evil (28:3; 92:8; 101:8) who lay traps to ensnare the just. But they are also those who go on the attack with violent acts, bloodthirsty (139:19) and deadly (17:9).

The actions attributed to the wicked also help define who they are. First of all, there are acts contrary to ethics. The wicked respect none of the elementary demands of justice: "The wicked borrow, and do not pay back" (37:21). They are motivated uniquely by desire for gain: "Such are the wicked;/ always at ease, they increase in riches" (73:12). When they speak, it is to bear false witness and sow hatred: "For wicked and deceitful mouths are opened against me,/ speaking against me with lying tongues./ They beset me with words of hate,/ and attack me without cause" (109:2-3). Above all, they put in cause the very life of the poor and the weak (11:2; 37:14).

But that's not all. Just as gravely aberrant is their attitude toward God. The psalms speak of their complacency and their refusal to seek God: "In arrogance the wicked persecute the poor. . . ./ For the wicked boast of the desires of their heart,/ those greedy for gain curse and renounce the LORD./ In the pride of their countenance the wicked say: 'God will not seek it out';/ all their thoughts are, 'There is no God'" (10:2-4; see also 10:13). Here wickedness appears as the result of a choice; even those who believe could become wicked if they refuse to seek God's will (119:155).

1. A. Chouraqui, *Les Psaumes* (Liminaires: Paris, P.U.F., 1979) 86ff.
2. E. Jenni and C. Westermann, *Theologisches Handwörterbuch zum Alten Testament,* vol. 2 (München: Chr. Kaiser Verlag, 1976) cols. 813–8.

Are the Psalms Too Violent?

The prayer of the psalms sometimes astonishes and even scandalizes us in the harshness of its sentences on the enemy. Such violent language seems in direct opposition to our evangelical teachings. There is no way to avoid the conflict. How can we consider as words of God the harsh language of some of the imprecatory passages (5:11; 18:35-43; 109:6-20; 137:7-9; etc.)?

The Divine Office solved the problem simply by eliminating almost all the verses that contain violent language. A few rare examples remain, such as in Psalm 118: "All the nations surrounded me;/ in the name of the LORD I cut them off!" (v. 10). But is avoiding most of these verses any real solution to the problem they pose? The danger, of course, is that we may find ourselves left with a liturgy that refuses to look reality in the face; which, in its desire to edify, refuses the job of confronting and resolving the violence and injustice in the world.

Even though we decry the violence of the imprecations, we must accept that it is there, in the Bible, and we must find some way to understand it.

Whether we like it or not, we must acknowledge that violence is a part of life in the world around us, but it is also *in* us. Although the psalms teach us to hope for all good things from God, they nevertheless do not ignore the harsh reality of our world as it is, and they quite naturally express strong indignation against all instances of injustice. Perhaps when we read these violent words, instead of taking them as dogma, we should question ourselves about our own responsibility for violence, and ask whether we are able to forgive our enemies.

A first reading of Psalm 109:6-19 makes it clear just how far a person can be brought by being exposed to injustice and attacks. But a closer look enables us to better understand what the psalmist is really expressing:

—It is not a blind and arbitrary expression of violence. On the contrary, we see that the psalmist has tried everything to make friends with the adversary (love, kindness, prayer; vv. 4-5).

—He recognized that his own response is excessive and awkward, acknowledging that he is wounded and upset: "For I am poor and needy,/ and my heart is pierced within me" (v. 22). There is no complacency here, no triumphalism in the violence of his words.

—He does not go around boasting like a Pharisee, claiming to be better than the others: he speaks of his fasting in terms that tell us of the effort he makes to control his own bad tendencies (v. 24).

—Finally, best of all, we notice that at the end of the psalm he has attained a degree of serenity (vv. 27-31), apparently having undergone some conversion as he prayed. What matters most in prayer is not how we feel when we start to pray, but how much our prayer has changed us.

WORD

DAVAR דבר

Davar	
Total OT	2,584
1. Jer	319
2. 1 Kgs	201
3. 2 Kgs	158
7. Ps	127

1. Root

Any study of the faith of Israel must necessarily include a look at the root *davar*. Indeed, the fundamental meaning of the experience at Sinai is illumined by a better comprehension of this word ("Then God spoke all these words," Exod 20:1; see also 20:19; 24:3-8). It is this root, also, that best describes the initial inspiring experience of the prophets (see Jer 1:4, 9, 12), which motivated their interventions in Israel's history.

Used as a verb (57x.), *davar* (to speak) has a meaning similar to or even the equivalent of the verb *ʾamar* (to say).

The noun *davar* (57x.) covers a whole gamut of concepts that the simple translation of word cannot begin to convey. It can mean the subject of one's talk (a matter; see Prov 11:13; 1 Kgs 15:5) or the actions of persons (see the titles of several prophetic books, such as Jeremiah and Amos). It can mean the summary given relative to each of the kings of Israel and Judah; it can be used to refer to an event, as in the Hebrew title of the book of Chronicles (literally, "words of the days"—in actuality, events in the national life of the Israelites). It can be found, also, in a set formula that marks the transition from one tale to the next: "And after these things . . ." (Gen 15:1; 22:1; etc.).

2. Usage

We could sum up the attitude of the prophets and sages toward *davar* in words reminiscent of the philosopher Blaise Pascal, speaking of "the greatness and the misery of the word." Unabashedly, the psalms list the many abuses of the word: lies, fraud and cheating, pride and arrogance, destruction, suffering and bitterness, or simply emptiness and meaninglessness (31:9; see also 5:7; 58:4; 63:12; 101:7).

Despite this unflattering picture of what happens in cases of abuse of the word, the psalmists nevertheless accord great importance to the value of the word in creation and in the maintenance of brotherly ties between individuals and between peoples. The value most often cited is justice: justice *(tsedeq),* the sense of justice *(mishpat),* uprightness *(mesharim),* and truth *(ʾemet).* "The mouths of the righteous utter wisdom,/ and their tongues speak justice" (37:30; see also 15:2-3).

Along with Genesis, the Psalter speaks of the creative power of the word of God in the beginning of the world: "By the word of the LORD the heavens were made,/ and all their host by the breath of his mouth" (33:6; see also 147:15, 18). Like the prophets, the psalmists express their deeply-held belief that God has spoken and continues to speak throughout the history of Israel: "He declares his word to Jacob,/ his statutes and ordinances to Israel" (147:19). He first spoke at Sinai (99:7), then in the desert (106:12). He continued to speak and to direct the history of Israel through the actions of the prophets, such as Samuel and Nathan (see 89:20).

Having evoked the collective experience of revelation, the psalmists immediately speak of the closeness of the word of God. God's word is close to all who believe and is the delight of the faithful: "In God, whose word I praise,/ in the LORD, whose word I praise,/ in God I trust; I am not afraid" (56:10-11). It is this word that guides the believer (119:105) and gives the faithful life (119:49-50).

ZION

TSION צִיּוֹן

Tsion	
Total OT	154
1. Isa	47
2. Ps	38
3. Jer	17

1. Root

Tsion is the ancient name for the hill in Jerusalem where the Jebusites had built their fortress. It lies between the valley of Cedron to the east and the valley of Tyropoeon to the west.

David took it by force (2 Sam 5:7), and the city of David was built and grew to the south of the hill of Zion. Although the name itself can stand for the entire city of Jerusalem and its population, it is rarely used to designate the political capital of Judah. We find Zion more in the context of the Temple (it is, in fact, the Temple mount, where David sets up an altar and where Solomon builds a temple), and for this reason it appears as the symbol of the dwelling-place of God, as well as of the City of God that is to come.

2. Usage

Mount Zion (2:6; 48:3, 12; 74:2; 78:68; 125:1; 133:3) is particularly dear to the heart of the psalmists. To them it is first and foremost a fortress, proud and impregnable, where the people will always find refuge in times of war and invasion: "Walk about Zion, go all around it,/ count its towers,/ consider well its ramparts;/ go through its citadels" (48:12-13).

Zion was also chosen by God to be God's dwelling place; it is where God wants to take up his abode: "For the LORD has chosen Zion;/ he has desired it for his habitation:/ 'This is my resting place forever;/ here will I reside, for I have desired it'" (132:13-14). For the psalmists the importance of Zion is not seen so much from a political as from a sacral point of view: it is a holy mountain, a sanctuary: "I have set my king on Zion, my holy hill" (2:6; see also 20:3). It is in Zion that the holy presence will be sought as the beloved object of the desires of generation upon generation, and as the goal of their pilgrimages: "Sing praises to the LORD, who dwells in Zion" (9:11; see also 76:3; 135:21). It is in Zion that they will find "his blessing, life forevermore" (133:3).

The image that the psalmists give us of Zion is deeply influenced by the tragic experience of the Exile, as well as by the wild hopes and longings to return once again to the holy mountain. Everyone knows the famous refrain, full of nostalgia, of Psalm 137: "By the rivers of Babylon—/ there we sat down and there we wept/ when we remembered Zion" (v. 1). Only a return to Zion, long cherished as an impossible dream (see 126:1), can bring back laughter and cries of joy: "O that deliverance for Israel would come from Zion!/ When God restores the fortunes of his people,/ Jacob will rejoice; Israel will be glad" (53:6).

Finally, the role of Zion is not limited to that of a national symbol. The psalmists also sing of Zion as the spiritual capital of humanity ("And of Zion it shall be said,/ 'This one and that one were born in it,'" 87:5), where peoples and nations will assemble at the end of time to acclaim God with a single voice: "Glorious things are spoken of you,/ O city of God./ Among those who know me I mention Rahab and Babylon;/ . . . Singers and dancers alike say,/ 'All my springs are in you'" (87:3-4, 7).

The Prayer of the Psalms: Seven Suggestions for Better Understanding

We have taken an in-depth look at a number of key words in the Psalter; following are some ideas offered in the hope that they might help the reader benefit as much as possible from praying the psalms. We shall look at the nature of the prayer of the psalms, composed so long ago, and ask ourselves how they can contribute to our own prayer today.

1. The Psalms as Dialogues (see Call [Cry out] and Word)

The recognition that the psalms express an ongoing, unceasing dialogue between God and the faithful is of paramount importance. Of course, the psalms are composed of human speech addressed to God, sometimes quite forcefully, but this is only half of the equation: we should never forget that in the psalms God is also speaking to us. In other words, the psalms are not monologues in which a human being talks on and on to God. On the contrary, the psalms suppose a previous dialogue that has already borne fruit. The psalmists were convinced that they could talk to God because God listened and paid attention to what they were saying. This is what we mean by saying that the psalms are based on a dialogue in which we see constant interaction between humanity crying out to God and the Lord who listens with benevolence and comes to our help. "Answer me when I call, O God of my right! / You gave me room when I was in distress. / Be gracious to me and hear my prayer. / . . . The Lord hears when I call to him" (4:1, 3).

This is what constitutes prayer: a true dialogue in which nothing that arises in the human heart is forbidden expression, a place where God can not only speak to us, but can intervene and deliver us from our distress. The psalmists would never have expressed all those passionate cries of anguish or joy if they had not believed they were heard by a God who listens and can be found through prayer.

We have to ask ourselves whether our prayer has become a monologue in which we have much to say, but in which we take precious little time to stop and see if God has something to say to us. What if the most important part of prayer is just this—God's response to us—and we do not hear it? God speaks in the psalms, often inviting us to change our ways. Again and again we are reminded that God is always there to help us, offering love and expressing the desire to see us take the path that leads to true happiness. So the real question we must ask about our way of praying is not whether we are saying the right things and truly expressing our lives to God, but if we are able to incorporate in our lives and truly live out what we hear every time we turn to God: "O that today you would listen to his voice!" (95:7).

2. The Psalms: Prayers of the Whole Body

There is something paradoxical about the fact that the psalms, which hold such an important place in both Jewish and Christian spirituality, are so concrete, so corporal, expressing as they do every possible human passion and posture of the body. Far from ignoring or denying the body, the prayer of the psalms arises from the eyes and the hands, with tears and groans, from the pain of the trembling body and the broken heart, but also from the joy of "bones which dance." Prayer is neither an abstract exercise nor a theological dissertation. There is no need to leave yourself behind and penetrate into a so-called spiritual realm in order to pray. All you have to do is speak out from where you find yourself, from your own experience. When we read the prayers of the psalmists, we can almost hear them breathe, groan, and exult; we sense their fear and discouragement, we hear their cries as they find themselves at the end of their rope, their throats dry, their eyes full of tears and their bones about to crumble to dust: "I am poured out like water,/ and all my bones are out of joint;/ my heart is like wax;/ it is melted within my breast;/ my mouth is dried up like a potsherd,/ and my tongue sticks to my jaws;/ you lay me in the dust of death" (22:14-15).

3. The Psalms Are Made to Be Sung to Music
(see Rejoice, Praise, Psalm)

The very word "psalm" means a piece of music. The heading of many psalms calls them a *mizmor*, from the verb *zamar*, which means to play music, to play a musical instrument. More than half the psalms (87 out of 150) are entitled *mizmor* or *shir*, which means song. So the psalms are musical pieces or songs. In addition to the headings, a number of psalms have other musical indications to show how they are to be performed. To ignore the musical character of the psalms is to lose a vital dimension and deprive them of the rhythm and vitality that gave rise to them and have ensured their popularity in both Jewish and Christian communities.

Besides the above-mentioned headings and notes about their performance, the psalms also contain many musical references within the text, some mentioning dancing as well: "Clap your hands, all you peoples;/ shout to God with loud songs of joy./ God has gone up with a shout,/ the LORD with the sound of the trumpet./ Sing praises to God, sing praises;/ sing praises to our King, sing praises./ For God is the king of all the earth;/ sing praises with a psalm" (47:1, 5-7; see also 98, 150).

It is strange that it seems so difficult to accompany the psalms with music in our Sunday liturgical celebrations. Often we give up entirely and simply recite the psalm, or we replace it with a more familiar and seemingly easier chant. And yet if there is one component of our worship that lends itself to full musical expression, it is the psalm. Even dance is part of this form of spontaneous, emotional prayer. Every available musical resource could be called in to play: trumpets and horns, drums and stringed instruments, flutes and cymbals. Singing and dancing could be used to express the joy or, conversely, the sorrow of the whole people. Why are we so timid and reserved in our use of the psalms? Could it be that we have not yet truly encountered the God of David and of the psalms, the Lord of the Dance?

4. The Simple Language of the Psalms

The idea for this small dictionary arose from the fact that the vocabulary of the psalms is really quite limited. Some forty or so words account for a large percentage of the psalm vocabulary. Biblical prayer is not afraid of repetition. We sing again and again of the greatness of God or of God's faithfulness or justice; we do not tire of expressing our joy at being able to speak with God and our confidence that we are heard.

So we see that the vocabulary of the Psalter is really very simple, taken from everyday life; there are no esoteric or elitist words. In the psalms we pray with the common language, with no artifice or fancy turns of phrase: "Incline your ear, O LORD, and answer me,/ for I am poor and needy./ Preserve my life, for I am devoted to you;/ save your servant who trusts in you./ You are my God; be gracious to me, O Lord,/ for to you do I cry all day long" (86:1-2).

There is nothing complicated in this, yet these simple words can speak for us in many different situations, expressing rich meanings and spiritual experiences of great power. Here again the psalms have a lesson for us: the authenticity of prayer only gains from an extreme simplicity of vocabulary, for repetition of basic feelings liberates the mind of the one who prays from all the nonessentials and keeps us focused on the one necessary purpose of prayer, which is to nourish the dialogue between God and us.

5. The Psalms as a Deep Look at Humanity
(See Soul, Flesh, Heart, Breath [Spirit], Human Being)

As we have already seen in our brief look at words such as soul, flesh, breath (spirit), and heart, the anthropology of the psalms is very different from that which has dominated Christian thinking in the West, much closer to the anthropology of the ancient Greeks. All of the above words, and others like them, were used to express the totality of the human being. According to the Bible, particularly in the Psalter, we are soul, flesh, and spirit. These realities are not separate entities, much less opposed parts of us, and they cannot be compartmentalized. They refer to the whole human being as seen from a particular angle.

A second aspect of how biblical language treats the human being is clear throughout the Psalter: we are spoken of in concrete terms, described through what it is we do. All of our activity is seen as taking place either in the heart (the interior part of the person), in our communication with one another (the realm of speech), or in our work (the work of our hands). In fact, there are a number of places in the Psalter where these three realms of human activity are mentioned together: "Who shall ascend the hill of the LORD? / And who shall stand in his holy place? / Those who have clean hands and pure hearts, / who do not lift up their souls to what is false, / and do not swear deceitfully" (24:3-4); "Deliver me, O LORD, from evildoers; . . ./ who plan evil things in their minds. . . ./ They make their tongue sharp as a snake's. . . ./ Guard me, O LORD, from the hands of the wicked" (140:1-4; see also 28:2-3; 37:30-31; 55:21-22). The fact that all these aspects of human life are presented in such close association underscores the unitary vision of the human being of the psalmists.

Finally, we can see in the psalms and in the Bible as a whole three distinct correspondences between aspects of the human being that put before us again and again the essential unity of the person. We see that the eyes reflect what is in the heart: "The precepts of the LORD are right, / rejoicing the heart; / the commandment of the LORD is clear, / enlightening the eyes" (19:8; see also 101:5; 131:1). In the same way, when the psalms speak of the word, they associate it with the parallel act of listening: "Hear a just cause, O LORD; / attend to my cry; / give ear to my prayer from lips free of deceit" (17:1; see also 4:2; 28:2; 54:4; 141:1). A third and last corresponding pair is the hands and the feet, which can symbolize between them a whole spectrum of actions (work, power, conquest, etc.): "[You] have not delivered me into the hand of the enemy; / you have set my feet in a broad place" (31:8; see also 36:12; 37:30-31).

6. The Psalms as Prayers of Conflict
(see the inserts "Those Problematic Enemies" and "Are the Psalms Too Violent?")

The world of the psalms is neither neutral nor naive. It is a world that knows conflict, battle, and strife. Indeed, the psalms that are entirely serene, in which there is not a trace of violence or a single allusion to the injustice that afflicts our world, are rare. The psalms speak of the violence and hatred of others. But they also express, either implicitly or openly, the violence that is in ourselves, certainly not edifying but undeniably present, even slipping insidiously into our prayer: "Rise up, O LORD, confront them, overthrow them!/ By your sword deliver my life from the wicked,/ from mortals—by your hand, O LORD—/ from mortals whose portion in life is in this world" (17:13-14); "But those who seek to destroy my life/ shall go down into the depths of the earth;/ they shall be given over to the power of the sword,/ they shall be prey for jackals" (63:9-10).

To pray the psalms is to be invited to take a long, hard look at the world as it is, threatened and often torn by violence. But in addition to looking outside of ourselves, we are also asked to examine our innermost being and bring ourselves just as we are into the merciful and loving presence of God, so that God might heal us of all our wounds and help us change those pockets of violence that slumber still in all of us into places of peace.

7. The Two Focal Words in the Prayer of the Psalms

Although the psalter does justice to all the cries that may burst from the lips of a human being there are two that sum up the whole of these prayers: "Help!" and "Alleluia!" While we may have the tendency to opt for one or the other, the prayer of the psalms contains both. Neither is prescribed in advance. They may arise successively within the same experience. But neither can be excluded from our prayer, because what is at stake is the true reality of God and that of the human being.

On the one hand the psalter is punctuated by cries for help: "make haste to help me, O Lord, my salvation!" (38:22); "O Lord, make haste to help me!" (40:14 and 70:1); "be gracious to me, O Lord!" (6:2); "be gracious to me, O Lord, for I am in distress" (31:9); "save me from all my pursuers, and deliver me!" (7:1); "save us, O Lord, our God!" (106:47). The prayer of the psalms is that of people who are suffering or are sensitive to the world's pain. It is a place in which to be conscience-stricken, but also a place in which we can speak out on behalf of those who suffer. All human pain deserves to be borne before God and be heard: that is the conviction at the heart of the innumerable cries of supplication that ring through the psalter.

But there is another word that is equally representative of the psalms: "Alleluia!" This cry, unknown to the other biblical books, defines the climate of biblical prayer better than any other word. Ideally every biblical prayer moves toward praise, as Paul Beauchamp has said so well: it is the alpha and omega, the beginning and end of biblical prayer (*Psaumes nuit et jour* [Paris: Editions du Seuil, 1980] 92). It can be no accident that this word is the last in the psalter. Prayer remains the ultimate vocation not merely for the people of the psalms, but for all creation: "Let everything that breathes praise the Lord. Alleluia!" (150:6).

Select Bibliography

Anderson, B. W. *Out of the Depths: The Psalms Speak for Us Today.* Rev. and expanded ed. Philadelphia: Westminster Press, 1983.

Brueggemann, W. *Abiding Astonishment: Psalms, Modernity, and the Making of History.* Louisville, Ky.: Westminster/John Knox Press, 1991.

_____. "Bounded by Obedience and Praise: The Psalms as Canon." *Journal for the Study of the Old Testament* 50 (1992) 63–92.

_____. *Israel's Praise: Doxology Against Idolatry and Ideology.* Philadelphia: Fortress Press, 1988.

_____. *The Message of the Psalms: A Theological Commentary.* Minneapolis: Augsburg Publishing House, 1984.

_____. *Praying the Psalms.* St. Mary's Press: Winona, Minn., 1984.

_____. "Psalms and the Life of Faith: A Suggested Typology of Function." *Journal for the Study of the Old Testament* 17 (1980) 3–32.

_____. "The Psalms as Prayer." *Reformed Liturgy and Music* 1:23 (1989) 13–26.

Craghan, J. F. *The Psalms: Prayers for the Ups, Downs and In-Betweens of Life: A Literary-Experiential Approach.* Wilmington, Del.: Michael Glazier, 1985.

Craven, T. *The Book of Psalms.* Collegeville: The Liturgical Press, 1992.

Holladay, W. L. *The Psalms Through Three Thousand Years: Prayerbook of a Cloud of Witnesses.* Minneapolis: Fortress Press, 1993.

Kraus, H. J. *Theology of the Psalms.* Trans. K. Crim. Minneapolis: Augsburg Publishing House, 1986.

Kselman, J. S., and M. L. Barré. "Psalms." *The New Jerome Biblical Commentary.* Ed. R. E. Brown, J. A. Fitzmeyer, and R. E. Murphy. Englewood Cliffs, N.J.: Prentice Hall, 1990.

McCann, J. C., Jr. "The Psalms as Instruction." *Interpretation: A Journal of Bible and Theology* 46 (1992) 117–28.

_____. *A Theological Introduction to the Book of Psalms: The Psalms as Torah.* Nashville: Abingdon Press, 1993.

Miller, P. D. *Interpreting the Psalms.* Philadelphia: Fortress Press, 1986.

Morse, M. *Psalms for Troubled Times.* Outremont: Novalis; Collegeville: The Liturgical Press, 1991.

Murphy, R. E. *The Psalms Are Yours.* New York; Mahwah, N.J.: Paulist Press, 1993.

Nowell, I. *Sing a New Song: The Psalms in the Sunday Lectionary.* Collegeville: The Liturgical Press, 1993.

Peterson, E. P. *Where Your Treasure Is: Psalms that Summon You from Self to Community.* Grand Rapids, Mich.: Eerdmans, 1993.

Pleins, J. D. *The Psalms: Songs of Tragedy, Hope, and Justice.* New York: Orbis Books, 1993.

Smith, M. S. "The Levitical Compilation of the Psalter." *Zeitschrift für die Alttestamentliche Wissenschaft* 103 (1991) 258–63.

_____. *Psalms: The Divine Journey.* New York: Paulist Press, 1987.

Westermann, C. *The Living Psalms.* Trans. J. R. Porter. Edinburgh: T & T Clark, 1989.

_____. *The Psalms: Structure, Content & Message.* Trans. R. D. Gehrke. Minneapolis: Augsburg Publishing House, 1980.